Scaling for Success

Scaling for Success

How to Build a Brand That Breaks Barriers

By Kathryn Strachan

Published by
Hybrid Global Publishing
333 E 14th Street
#3C
New York, NY 10003

Manufactured in the United States of America, or in the United Kingdom when distributed elsewhere.

Strachan, Kathryn
Scaling for Success: How to Build a Brand That Breaks Barriers
    Print Book: 978-1-961757-81-3
    E Book: 978-1-961757-82-0

Cover design by: Julia Kuris
Copyediting by: Sue Toth
Interior design by: Suba Murugan
Author Photographer: Gabriel Niedojadlo

This book is for all marketing managers, CMOs and company founders building a brand. Whether you're building a brand from the ground up or looking to unlock the next stage of growth, you'll find the insights you need within these pages.

Getting Started

I remember picking a name—the first thing any business needs—with a friend of mine. I had reached the point where my freelance businesses needed to be registered as an Ltd. and, therefore, needed a name. We batted around ideas trying to land on a name and explored everything from silly names like 'Copy Train' to names focused on me, like 'Kathryn Strachan Ltd.' While many freelancers opt for names like the latter, I wanted to build a company that others could stand behind, as one day I might make it big and have employees.

I knew I wanted a team, so I wanted to choose a name that everyone could believe in, and that would serve as the foundation for what was to come. It was my first step in building a brand.

But a name is just a name until you put something behind it. It's the messaging, ethos, values, and everything else that goes into building a brand that makes a name really special and something worth talking about. This is the story of how CopyHouse became more than just a name and how I've helped countless companies do the same ever since.

★★★

One of the first things people ask me is what motivated me to start an agency. The truth is, I'm not sure I meant to … not exactly. …

I had been working as a contractor at Scottish Widows, reporting every day to my corporate job but feeling the soul-crushing impact of corporate politics and not being able to create real, lasting change. The corporate world, in general, requires so many hoops to jump through before any creativity can come to life—so much so that over my eight months as a copywriter at Scottish Widows, nothing I had written had ever made it to the website, as it would eventually die a death in procurement or legal.

I dreamed of creating something from scratch and having a real, lasting impact. So, despite not having an extensive background in marketing or a little black book of clients, I struck out on my own to build an agency and use the nest egg I had saved from my time at Scottish Widows to hire my first employees.

At the time, I didn't know I was building an agency, let alone a brand. I simply wanted to harness my copywriting skills to create awesome content and knew that I couldn't do it alone. I needed a team that I could train and bring on the journey with me.

While many agencies rely on a pool of freelancers, I knew that I wanted to have an in-house team that I could really invest in and, in turn, have them believe in the company. I wanted to surround myself with a team that was as passionate about CopyHouse as I was and who could help me build a brand to be proud of and feel truly invested in.

In many ways, that hasn't changed, and we still keep most of our work in-house today.

So, in January 2020, I made my first few hires—bringing on board an account manager, copywriter, and social media manager. Little did I know how drastically the world would change just a few months later with the outbreak of a global pandemic.

When COVID hit in March 2020, we were a scrappy team of four, having just moved out of a co-working space and into a brand-new office. I had signed the lease on the Monday before we entered lockdown. Needless to say, my timing wasn't great.

At the time, we worked with clients across travel, recruitment, technology, and financial services. I was new to running an agency, and we didn't have any contracts or safeguards in place, which meant that our clients could leave with little to no notice. Unfortunately for us, many did, especially that first week. Overnight, we lost almost 60 percent of our clients and were left with very few.

But I had just made my first hires and felt so passionate about the work we were doing. I didn't want to make anyone redundant or furlough anyone. So, instead, I looked hard at the clients we had left, what we did well, and how we could compete against other agencies. What was the one thing we could do that could set us apart?

I saw that we did a lot in the technology sector, and few other agencies worked in this space. It was hard and complicated and far from sexy industries like travel or hospitality. But it was an area with a big need, as technology companies desperately needed to tell their stories in a way that wasn't dry, dull, or jargon-heavy. It was also an area that could survive and thrive during a global pandemic.

So, I secured the bounce-back loan and used it to invest in our sales, marketing, and business advisory to truly build a brand and allow us to slingshot outside of the pandemic. Good race car drivers know that they need to slow down around corners so they can zip past competitors and this was exactly the approach I channeled to set the foundations for our sky-high impressive growth.

Since then, we've grown from that scrappy team of four to a 25-person team with a turnover above £1.5 million (something only 3 percent of agencies achieve). It's not always been an easy route, and I've certainly made mistakes and learned some valuable lessons along the way. I've learned how to hire a marketing team, invest properly in marketing, and create a community of marketing managers and CMOs. Our growth is almost entirely due to the strong brand we've built and all the opportunities it has unlocked as a result.

Today, I help technology companies that are facing similar challenges. Many have impressive track records and have operated for decades. But they haven't invested properly in their marketing and have instead relied on word of mouth and referrals. However, this growth model isn't reliable, and they hit a glass ceiling where they aren't hitting their growth targets and certainly aren't growing as quickly as they'd like. At this point, they realize they need to invest in brand building to not only stand out from the crowd but to create inbound leads and unlock the next level of growth.

Join me as I explore the lessons learned from growing my agency and share insights to help you start the journey of building a brand.

Chapter 1

Defining Your Market Positioning

Before you can start building a brand, you need to create the right foundations. Setting the right foundations will ensure you're headed in the right direction before you spend too much money or time going down the wrong path. It's much harder to change tracks later on if you decide to drastically change your positioning, and you would be facing the uphill battle of already being recognized for your initial positioning.

Step one in building a brand is to set the right foundations by identifying and defining your market positioning. In other words, what will you be known for, by whom, and why?

Over the years, I've met many brands that have struggled to define their market positioning. Should they choose a specific niche or remain generalist—especially if their product could technically be sold to everyone? Should they focus on one industry or be industry-agonistic? Should they focus on one product or embrace a more comprehensive approach? Surely, keeping these options as broad as possible would create the most opportunities and allow them to attract the greatest number of sales.

I believe that failing to create a clear position is one of the biggest mistakes you can make when building a brand.

WHY DEFINING YOUR MARKET POSITIONING IS IMPORTANT

I spend a lot of my time networking and building relationships, so I meet many, many brands. One of the first questions I always ask is, "What do you do?" As a result, I have heard a lot of positioning statements. How people explain what they do tells me a lot about how well a brand understands its positioning.

The conversation often goes like this:

"What do you do?"

"We're a full-service digital marketing agency working across all industries."

Or

"We're a technology provider that offers comprehensive, industry-agnostic solutions."

These answers are problematic for many reasons. First of all, unless you have a massive team, big marketing budgets, and established reach, it's highly unlikely that you cover all services or solutions equally well. It's also unlikely that you've worked across all industries and if you do, that you understand all industries.

It's also problematic because it doesn't help me understand how to help you. It's estimated that the average adult makes around 35,000 decisions every day. To make so many decisions, we need to compartmentalize, which helps us store information, understand how to react, and make these decisions without becoming overwhelmed. This basic element of human psychology explains the need for clear positioning.

If your brand doesn't clearly fit into a category, it will be much harder for people to process and remember you later on.

Whom do I introduce you to? What opportunities would be right for you? Where do you really excel, and where can I rely on you to deliver expertise?

So, while being a generalist may seem like it would create more opportunities, this isn't entirely true. It ultimately creates confusing messaging that makes it almost impossible for anyone, even those with the best intentions, to actually help you.

You Don't Sell to Everyone

When defining your market positioning, it's important to understand your audience, as "what you do" is only half the equation. You also need an audience that's willing to buy your product or solution and that you can rely on to create brand advocates who'll champion you even when you're not in the room.

As part of understanding your market position, you'll also need to develop an understanding of your ideal audience, how this relates to your brand, and how you can use these insights to develop very clear messaging.

However, sometimes I meet a brand that believes it can sell to everyone. "But everyone can use our product," I hear them protest.

This isn't exactly true, as not everyone could, or should, use your product. Even the biggest brands don't sell to everyone. Your grandmother is unlikely to be the ideal audience for a metaverse Oculus headset (no offense, Granny). Your product or solution will be more attractive to some audiences than others, and you may even have specific business reasons for focusing on one audience; for example, do some customers have a higher cost of acquisition or lower retention rates? Do some not align with your core values or future vision for the company?

If you're working in the technology industry, you may also need to consider Rodger's wave of adoption, depending on how cutting-edge your product or solution is. For very cutting-edge technologies, you might be looking for early adopters, who are more comfortable with risk and enjoy using emerging products (even if the use cases aren't there yet or they aren't fully developed), while more mature technology might rely on laggards or late adopters or need to look at other ways to unlock new audiences.

Regardless, it's almost impossible for you to sell to everyone. Understanding the audience your product or solution most appeals to and going after this audience will help you greatly in setting the right foundations.

Standing Out From the Competition

Having a strong position is even more important in oversaturated industries, especially if you offer similar products or services. For example, open banking companies often have this problem as open banking solutions are largely the same, and standing out requires developing a strong proposition.

Begin by looking at the competitive landscape. What do you do that your competitors don't? How do they describe their product or solutions and how can you position your company as different? Is there a certain industry or vertical that you can champion to narrow down the competition?

Identifying a unique advantage that's easy to communicate in one or two sentences will make a massive difference when operating within an overly saturated market.

HOW TO DEVELOP YOUR POSITIONING

So, now that you understand the value of having clear positioning, how exactly do you develop your positioning? Where do you begin?

Keep. It. Simple.

When defining your positioning, it's always best to start with one question:

If you could be known for one thing, what would it be?

Or, in other words, where can you sink your flag and really claim it as yours? What do you do better than anyone else, and why should your customers choose you?

When I decided to narrow our focus to the technology industry, I did this by looking at what we did very well and where my personal expertise lay. During my master's program in modern literature at UCL, I loved diving into more technical concepts and once wrote an essay on complex theories of time in *Alice* in *Wonderland* and the riddles Lewis Carrol hid in the text. So, when working as a freelance copywriter, I naturally embraced some of the more complex subjects and built the early days of my career at the desk of Scottish Widows. Having come from a more technical background, I understood the need for good copy in these industries and also knew it was something others really struggled to deliver. It was the one thing we could be known for, and it continues to shape my company today.

I've seen firsthand the benefits of focusing on one key strength and, as such, am a big believer in doing one thing really well. It allows you to simplify your messaging and to make it clear what you do and for whom. Of course, as you grow, you can expand your core focus and extend your capabilities. But remember, the more you want to be known for, the more you'll need to invest to build brand awareness and market credibility around this capability.

Conduct Market Research

While you could choose a niche or market segment that's already popular or oversaturated, it'll be much harder. Now, if you have an unlimited marketing budget and resources, you might be able to compete with those already dominating the space.

But, if, like most brands, you don't have deep pockets or unlimited resources, you'll want to find a market segment that isn't already saturated. Given the current markets in the US and UK, it's highly unlikely that you'll offer a truly unique solution and not have any competitors.

Once you have identified target markets, conduct research into who else already works in these industries. Whom will you be competing against? Do they already have strong brands? What can you offer that they don't? How will you stand out?

When I defined CopyHouse's focus on the technology industry, I started by conducting market research on who was already in the field. At the time, there weren't many agencies that were delivering content for the technology industry, which gave us a good opportunity to stand out. We were also hearing from clients and prospects who were struggling to find providers who could create content on complex topics like blockchain, NFTs, metaverse, etc. You can't just wake up and write about blockchain so having clear expertise and an existing understanding of these industries allowed us to quickly get up to speed with new clients and also deliver the quality of content they were looking for.

Not only do you need to identify the one thing you do better than anyone else, but also how can you stand out against those already dominating in that space.

How to Conduct Market Research

When conducting market research for my consulting clients, I start by asking them for the top five competitors (normally, they'll know this as these are the brands they lose clients to) and also look at the brand's ranking on page 1 for my client's core services or products.

I then look at the messaging on their websites and marketing activities to identify how they talk about their company (i.e., how they position themselves) as well as their more general marketing activities. How often do they publish articles, and on what topics? What social media channels are they active on? Who appears to be their main audience?

This light desk research often reveals how they position themselves, where the gaps might be in the market, and how my clients can gain a competitive advantage.

To Niche or Not to Niche

One way to cut through the noise is to focus on specific industries or verticals. Focusing on specific industries allows you to pare down the number of competitors. While there may be many digital agencies, there aren't many (or as many) specifically targeting the technology industry.

Choosing the right industries to target can often seem like an insurmountable challenge. It might mean needing to part with certain clients that don't fit within this niche or seem to limit new opportunities by narrowing your focus. However, as the saying goes, "The narrower the focus, the deeper the cut," and I've certainly found this to be true.

Having a niche not only gives you a stronger focus but also allows you to really champion and become known in one industry. It's much easier to establish your expertise within a specific industry and position yourself as the go-to company.

Focusing on the technology industry has been massively helpful in CopyHouse's growth. By niching into the technology industry, I was able to direct the budget to the right places and quickly establish our expertise with CMOs and marketing managers at technology brands. It's allowed us to punch above our weight and attract large clients, like Meta and Klarna, almost from the get-go. It's shaped everything we do, from who we hire, the systems we use, and most importantly, how we've built a brand and what we've become known for.

Identify Your Target Industry

Now that we've recognized that you don't sell to everyone, the next step is to identify whom you sell to. One way to do this is to look at who you currently work with or, in other words, where you already have case studies.

It's sensible to start with industries and audiences where you already have case studies, as building credibility in an entirely new industry is a lot harder and will definitely take longer. However, that's not to say it's impossible if you're building from scratch or really feel it's essential to pursue a new space.

Start by mapping out the industries of your current clients. Where do you have the most clients? Do these industries have a role to play in your company's future? Can you leverage your past experiences and customer testimonials to attract more clients in these industries?

With CopyHouse, I saw that we already did a lot of work within the technology industry. Due to the pandemic, our clients in other industries, like travel and recruitment, had been wiped out, which, perhaps fortunately, allowed me to clearly see where we had strong case studies and examples we could leverage to attract more clients within the tech space.

Create a Target List

While it's always helpful to look at your past experiences and track record, it's also equally important to look forward by identifying the industries you want to be part of. If you could work with anyone, who would it be and why? In what industries do you see the most growth or potential?

I often recommend that clients start by creating a target list or dream list of brands they'd love to work with and then examining this list for any similarities. Do these brands operate within a similar space? What do they have in common? Do they all operate within a similar geography or industry, or even have a similar need?

This list can also serve for account-based marketing (ABM) research and give you the opportunity to really understand what makes your targeted brands tick. For example, do they cover B2B and B2C industries and are likely to need a provider that does both? Do they work exclusively in the US and need a provider in this market?

You can then use these insights to shape your positioning statement to reflect their perfect solution and some of the key traits they might be looking for. You can also use these more future-focused insights and pair them with your past track record to find your sweet spot and ultimate market position.

CREATING A BASIC POSITIONING STATEMENT

By doing this research and reflection, you ultimately want to get to a position where you can confidently say what you do and for whom. For example, a basic positioning statement might look like the following:

"A global content marketing agency helping build brand awareness for technology companies."

You want one or two sentences that encompass what you do, for whom, and why. While these statements can take many forms, if you're stuck, you can use the following formula:

We help X achieve Y by offering X.

YOUR POSITIONING CAN CHANGE OVER TIME, AND AS YOU DO

Many companies are intimidated or overwhelmed by creating a clear positioning statement because they think that once defined, it'll be set in stone. What if they want or need to pivot later down the line? Wouldn't this limit their ability to do so?

However, this isn't entirely true.

While it can certainly be difficult to switch tracks, the level of difficulty will depend on the extent of the changes. Typically speaking, your positioning can, will, and should evolve as your company does.

I often meet companies that haven't looked at their messaging for years or decades. They may have set their positioning and all the surrounding messaging at the beginning of the company's establishment and then parked it in a drawer to gather dust. As a result, it no longer fits them and isn't fit for purpose.

Instead, I recommend continually reviewing your positioning and messaging to ensure that they still reflect your company and your goals.

Take, for example, CopyHouse's messaging. It's certainly changed over time—as we've adapted who we wanted to target, the markets we operated in, and the services we offered.

When we first created our positioning statement, it read something like, "A copywriting agency for B2B fintech and technology companies."

However, as we grew, we expanded our services to include social media and design, so pivoting away from a copywriting agency to a content marketing agency gave us greater scope.

We also made some mistakes along the way, like including two sectors in our proposition, which meant people naturally thought of us only for fintech. This wasn't quite right and definitely not the impression we wanted to make, as we've always worked across the tech sector.

We also discovered that most of our ideal brands operated in B2B and B2C, so we would naturally want an agency that could offer both. Limiting ourselves to only B2B could make us less attractive to our target audience. That's why customer research and considering your audience are so important.

Today, our positioning isn't a million miles away from where we originally started, but it has changed to allow us to attract our ideal clients and refine what we're known for.

Chapter 2

Identifying Your Audience and Leveraging Emotive Marketing

I'm a strong believer in the power of understanding your audience and using those insights to shape and lead your marketing strategy. All good marketing strategies should start with your audience.

Your audience will determine your overall approach, including how much budget is required, what channels you should be active on, and even what topics you should talk about. It all stems from your audience, as the entire point of marketing is to build relationships and kick-start important conversations.

Without this understanding and perspective, any relationship will be entirely one-sided. This is how and why you meet brands that only talk about how great their product is and the granular features and forget about their audience. Understanding your audience allows you to make better decisions and justify your reasoning.

So, it's hardly surprising that I always start building a marketing strategy by defining the customer avatars. Without detailed profiles that identify pain points, your marketing will be directionless—like a ship adrift at sea—and you'll seriously struggle to build brand awareness.

WHY UNDERSTANDING YOUR AUDIENCE IS IMPORTANT

"If you're trying to reach everyone, you'll reach no one."

Without a strong understanding of your audience, your messaging will lack a punch and will likely fall on deaf ears. You'll often see this represented as generic vanilla copy that lacks any emotions, empathy, or strong hooks. Generic copy is like being in a crowded room and saying, "Hey, everyone," to try to get the crowd's attention. Nine times out of ten, no one will pay you any attention and will continue with their busy days and schedules.

How often have you walked by the person handing out leaflets on the street? Probably almost every time, as it's not relevant to you.

However, when you understand your audience, your messaging is personalized and designed to cut through the noise to attract attention. Now, your messaging shifts from being generic to making people sit up and pay attention as they think you're speaking directly to them. Instead of saying, "Hey, everyone," you're suddenly saying, "Hey, man wearing the blue shirt," and all the men wearing blue shirts will turn around and look at you as if they believe you're speaking to them.

How often have you been with your child in a store and heard someone say, "Hey, Mom," and turned around expecting to see your loved one? This is the power of personalized messaging.

When you understand your audience, you can craft messaging that makes them sit up and pay attention. You secure their trust as you show them that you understand them, their challenges, and what's keeping them awake at night. Since you understand, you can offer them a solution that addresses their unique pain points. Taking the time to understand your audience and then harnessing these insights ultimately allows you to build relationships that foster trust and loyalty and position you as the *only* brand that can solve their problems.

WHAT ARE BUYER PERSONAS?

Most marketers are familiar with buyer personas in some form. Buyer personas often go by many different names: ICPs (ideal customer personas), customer avatars, customer personas, etc. But ultimately, they all mean essentially the same thing—a detailed profile of your audience and what makes them tick.

In its simplest form, a buyer persona should capture all the information you need to put yourself in your audience's shoes.

Many marketers build buyer personas by simply looking at the data in their systems and then don't take it any further. While these insights can be helpful for data segmentation or prospecting, the data from your CRM system won't tell you enough about the psychological triggers and pain points that make buyer personas useful. After all, knowing the job title, location, or age bracket of your buyer persona isn't enough to secure their trust and effectively position yourself as a brand that understands them.

Perhaps one of the biggest criticisms of buyer personas is that they're not helpful and are limited in the insights they offer. When buyer personas aren't created properly, they're likely to be ignored and sit in a drawer gathering dust. However, when done properly, they allow you to unlock a new level of empathy and emotions that make your marketing truly effective.

To achieve this, good buyer personas need to go much, much deeper than surface-level demographic information by looking at the paint points and psychological elements that influence how people make decisions. What's keeping your audience awake at 2 am? What are they worried about? What are they experiencing in the days, weeks, or months leading up to looking for a solution? How can you help them overcome their challenges? And how can you, perhaps more importantly, convert them into customers that use and love your product?

EMOTIVE MARKETING IN B2B

Historically, B2B marketers have struggled to embrace a more emotive approach to marketing. After all, they're selling to businesses rather than humans, so they shouldn't need the same level of emotional understanding as B2C marketers, right?

I've worked with many B2B companies, as that's the area CopyHouse primarily works within, so I have heard many reasons why B2B marketers *shouldn't* use emotional marketing. Many worry that this approach won't be taken seriously and that they'll struggle to get buy-in from CFOs and CEOs.

But over the years, I've become a big advocate and believer in emotional marketing in B2B. In fact, I think emotions often run higher at work than they do at home. So, yes, psychology and emotions play a large role in effective B2B marketing.

When was the last time you were awake worrying about something? I'd almost bet that you were worried about something related to work—perhaps a project that hadn't quite gone right or an approaching hard deadline. When we spend more than a third of our life at work (and the other third asleep), it's not surprising that our work lives cause more stress than our personal lives, and as such, we often require more support, reassurance, and help at work.

The decisions we make at work are more likely to have far greater consequences than the purchasing decisions we make in our personal lives. B2B buying decisions typically take six to 12 months and have a much higher purchasing price. Making the wrong decision could result in financial, reputational, or even professional loss—which is where the saying, "No one gets hired for hiring IBM," comes from—and is often far harder to reverse. In B2C, if you buy the wrong pair of shoes, it's easy to return them and get your money back, but in B2B, if you choose the wrong technology stack, you could be stuck with legacy technology for years or suffer a data leak that seriously damages your company.

With B2B marketing, you also have to juggle the sometimes competing needs of multiple stakeholders, some of whom you may never meet and all of whom have their own concerns, stresses, and needs. For example, your main contact might be a CMO, but they still need to secure buy-in from the CFO or CEO. Catering to these players' emotional states is still important for building trust and credibility, even if they're not in the room.

These complexities and others stress the importance of understanding your audience and leveraging emotional marketing—even in B2B marketing. If we don't take the time to create buyer personas that go beyond surface-level details, we risk alienating these audiences and not giving them the information they need to feel supported and confident in their buying decisions.

Thankfully, I've seen that attitudes toward emotive content in B2B changed during the pandemic. Before, we had a clear divide between work and personal life, which made it easier to overlook individuals' emotional states while at work. However, the lockdown forced our personal and professional lives together, meaning it was no longer possible to leave "it at the door," and companies needed to think about and support employees' mental health at work. We suddenly saw individuals as humans both at work and at home.

Marketers have embraced this trend by creating campaigns that play into these emotions and help build more personalized relationships between brands and their audience—something that I believe is essential for a brand's success. I've seen it firsthand while building the community around CopyHouse—our supporters have become friends, co-workers, clients, and so much more.

HARNESSING PAIN POINTS

Pain points are the first step toward creating more emotive marketing and, as such, should be an essential ingredient for any buyer persona. Pain points help you understand your audience's challenges, mental state, and key priorities, as these challenges need to be solved immediately—they cannot wait. Pain points are a marketer's secret weapon, and if you can tap into them, you can create a sense of urgency and importance around your product or service.

I explain it a bit like the difference between a pain reliever and a vitamin. Without understanding your audience's pain points, your product or solution is a vitamin—something "nice to have" that can wait till next month, next quarter, or even next year. It doesn't need to happen now.

But when you can effectively leverage pain points, you become far more important and business-critical. Rather than being a vitamin, you become a pain reliever, and your product or service becomes an "urgent need." If you have a headache, you're not going to wait till next month to take a pain reliever—you'll take it as soon as you're physically able. You need it right now, without delay.

Understanding your audience and their pain points and adapting your messaging accordingly is essential for unlocking growth and building brand awareness.

One of the very first things I did when building CopyHouse was to sit down and identify our audience, what their lives were like, and how we could help them the most. Then, every piece of content and marketing effort could be targeted exactly at them. While these personas have changed over time as we've gone from working with smaller brands with founder-led marketing to larger brands with CMOs, staying focused on our audience has allowed us to effectively prioritize our efforts and make sure we were devoting resources to the right areas. The times we've made the wrong decisions, it's been because we weren't focused on solving our audience's challenges.

How to Harness Pain Points

When you understand your audience's pain points, it becomes much easier to create content that cuts through the noise and allows you to show a level of understanding. You understand—heck, even feel—your audience's pain and are able to offer them a solution that truly solves their problems and provides tangible benefits, thereby moving away from being feature-driven to being benefit-driven. Your product doesn't process invoices five times faster; it allows an overstretched finance manager to make it home for dinner with their family.

It also helps you understand the messages your audience needs to hear and those they don't. Rather than over-inflated websites with thousands of pages, you can identify the content they need and pare down the user journey to offer a more streamlined process. After all, if someone is in pain, they don't want to wade through thousands of pages to find the solution.

By addressing pain points, you can offer helpful, meaningful advice that allows you to meet your audience where they are and take them on a journey toward ultimately becoming your biggest brand advocate.

Selling Benefits, Not Features

One of the most common symptoms of not focusing on the audience's pain points is when brands try to sell their product by features rather than benefits. The feature-driven approach fails to notice and address the audience's pain points and how the product helps solve their challenges. Rather, it focuses internally on the elements product teams find most important. Unfortunately, this is quite common with tech companies, especially tech companies that may be in the early days of their marketing journey.

I understand why it happens. When you've spent months or even years building a product, it's easy to be so impressed with its functionality and what it does. After all, you've spent a significant amount of time and overcome many challenges to create that feature—which is great—but your audience doesn't care or certainly not in the same way.

It comes back to the why rather than the what or how. Why is that feature important? Why is it essential to your offering? Most importantly, why should your audience care?

Tapping into your audience's pain points is one of the easiest ways to begin to think from the customer's perspective and transition from being feature-driven to being benefit-driven. Achieving this shift is no small feat but is essential for developing your approach to marketing and embracing a more empathetic approach that allows you to become more external facing. When you are truly external facing and clued into your audience, it becomes much easier to build a strong community of loyal brand advocates that help to champion your product and significantly increase your brand awareness.

BUILDING BUYER PERSONAS

Now that you understand the value of buyer personas, how do you actually go about building them? Where do you begin, and how do you create personas that you can actually use?

One of the best ways to begin is by hosting a half-day workshop and getting all the key stakeholders in the same room. While you don't want too many cooks in the kitchen, it's helpful to have senior leaders from sales, marketing, customer service, etc. to contribute their insights and find common ground. The workshop is essentially your opportunity to set the hypothesis of what they think their buyers are like. Later, you'll need to test this hypothesis by conducting interviews and speaking with clients, but we'll explore that a little farther on in the book.

We often help clients build buyer personas by running half-day workshops, but you can also lead your company through this exercise. However, make sure to take a wider view and act as a facilitator to guide your team members through the session. Hold off contributing your thoughts until the analysis. Also, make sure to be aware of and avoid the information gap.

Overcoming the Information Gap

One of the challenges of running the workshop internally is falling into the information gap.

Information gaps occur when you spend so long fully immersed in a topic that you can only see it from your perspective and mistakenly believe that everyone understands the topic as you do. This is quite common within companies as you spend a large majority of your time speaking with your coworkers and surrounded by people who also intimately know the company and product. For example, you may use acronyms or jargon with your day-to-day work that have become second nature but customers don't use or understand. If it takes new employees time to get up to speed on your lingo, it can be a good indication of information gaps within a company.

Recently, I met a friend for lunch. He has quite an impressive background in the fintech world and has just come from a meeting with a big bank. He was quite perplexed as, during the meeting, the representative from the bank had kept using the term OD and he had no idea what this was. He could guess it probably meant overdraft but couldn't ask directly. This is an example of an information gap and how it might lead customers astray or leave them feeling like your technology is too complicated or doesn't meet their needs (when it very well could).

It's highly unlikely that your audience will understand your product or area of expertise as well as you do. Even when you're selling into the C-suite, they won't know the inner workings of your product like you do. That would be nearly impossible when you have years of experience working with the company or that niche area of the industry.

As marketers, it's our job to take these insights and deliver them to your audience in a way they will understand. This starts with understanding where your audience currently is and identifying how we can convey these messages to them. Sometimes, you need an external perspective to see the forest from the trees.

Identifying Your Ideal Buyer Persona

Before you can create buyer personas, you need to identify who you're targeting or envisioning.

I normally recommend thinking about your ideal or best buyer. If you could work with anyone, who would it be? Who would be your perfect or dream customer? It's okay if you don't already work with these individuals, as this is relatively common, especially if you're just getting started or are looking at your next stage of growth.

Ideal buyer personas are all about whom you'd *ideally* like to work with, and this may not be your current client base. You may choose to focus more on aspirational personas, and that's totally fine. In fact, I'd encourage you to focus on capturing your ideal audience so you can align your messaging and marketing instead of focusing on an audience that no longer serves your business.

You may approach this from a commercial perspective and consider the buyers who create the most profit, have the lowest cost of acquisition, or have the highest retention rates. If you're a purpose-driven organization, you might choose to focus on people who align with your values or ethos.

You might also consider creating personas for:

- **Key decision-makers.** Who might influence or control the decisions of your main point of contact? These are often more behind-the-scenes individuals.
- **Anti-buyer personas.** Whom do you absolutely hate working with? What are some of their characteristics? Identifying these individuals can help you avoid problematic customers and build relationships with the wrong people.
- **Internal stakeholders.** If you work in a larger organization and need to get buy-in from *your* internal stakeholders or need to navigate the tricky field of office politics, creating stakeholder profiles can be helpful.

While there may be many, many stakeholders you could create personas for, I typically recommend starting with two to three personas. Two or three tends to be a good number for getting started as it gives you a variety of stakeholders to center your marketing around without overwhelming or stretching budgets and resources too thin. Keep in mind that each persona will require their own content and marketing strategy, so while you can certainly create more personas, you'll need to make sure your marketing efforts align. Do you have enough money and time to effectively market to and build relationships with five or six different personas?

Getting Started: Top-Level Demographics

When building buyer personas, it's often easier to start with top-level demographics like name, location, gender, etc. We often already know some of these details as we've worked with and interacted with our audience previously.

What are some of the top-level characteristics of your buyer personas? What are we going to call them? Feel free to give them a funny name to bring a bit of humor to the process.

You'll typically look to define:

Name:
Age:
Gender:
Where they live:
Annual income:
Occupation:

This information essentially sets the stage before we dive into the deeper psychological elements. It'll also help you data in your CRM system, target prospects on social media, and tackle some of the more surface-level marketing activities.

Getting Started: World Beliefs

After we've identified some of the top-level characteristics, it's often a good idea to consider your personas' worldviews and beliefs. These beliefs will shape how they behave during the purchasing process and how they ultimately interact with your brand.

For example, are they risk-averse and like to look at the finer details? Are they dreamers and more into the big picture? What does their worldview look like? What's their attitude?

I normally ask workshop attendees to try to list at least three to five core life beliefs. We then use these beliefs to set the stage for the deeper, darker psychological elements.

Diving Deeper: Deep and Dark

Once you've set the stage, the next step is to take a deeper dive into who these individuals are, what makes them tick, and, most importantly, what they're awake at 2 a.m. thinking about. What's worrying them, and what are their fears about the product or service they're about to buy? This is where we really get into the juicy stuff that'll allow you to put yourself in their shoes and leverage emotive marketing.

When we address this session in workshops, we ask our clients to put themselves quite literally in their audiences' shoes by answering the questions via role-play. It helps them practice seeing things from another perspective and feel more connected to their buyer personas.

During this stage, we encourage our clients to think about the following questions in relation to the product or service they're selling:

- What does your audience secretly fear may be true about their lives? How do those fears relate to the service/product they're about to buy?
- What keeps them up at night?
- Where will you lose power, influence, and control in your life if things don't change or if they get worse?
- What do they wish companies/brands/providers in this industry understood about them?

Role-playing these answers helps uncover some interesting insights into the psychology behind your audience. Remember, here we're simply aiming to set a hypothesis and capture your thoughts on what you think the problems and challenges your audience has. We'll need to test these insights to ensure you're not making incorrect assumptions. Or, as my mother used to say, "making an ass out of you and me."

Diving Deep: High as the Sky

After you've explored the deep and dark side, it's important to look at the other side of the coin. What are your audience's dream solutions? This gives us the opportunity to consider *how* you might solve their challenges and essentially align your product or service to your audience's needs. How can you create a solution that exceeds expectations and becomes an almost no-brainer?

When we run this session in the workshop, we also use the role-play technique to envision your buyer personas' mentality and help them solve their challenges. We might consider asking questions like:

- What's the dream solution they'd pay almost anything for?
- What will they get or achieve if their fantasy situation comes true?
- What specific difference do they hope to make in their lives?

Of course, it's important to think about these dream solutions in relation to your business and products or services. How can we truly help your audience? Where is the value in what you do?

This is your chance to understand the value you offer and find the messaging that will inspire your audience (and maybe even yourself).

Test Your Assumptions

During the workshop, your aim is to capture the insights from your coworkers and internal stakeholders. However, these insights serve only to create a hypothesis of who *you* think your audience is. Your assumptions will be influenced by your perceptions, which, of course, only tell one side of the story. It's impossible to ensure these insights are 100 percent correct without verifying them.

The best way to verify your hypothesis is by conducting interviews with individuals who match the top-level demographics. I recommend interviewing at least three individuals for each of the personas. These individuals should match top-level demographics, such as job titles for B2B marketers or location, gender, and age for B2C marketers. While this won't ensure complete consistency, it's easier to identify people based on top-level demographics than deeper, darker psychological elements.

Ideally, you'll interview current clients or customers as well as individuals you haven't yet worked with. You can source these individuals via social media, like LinkedIn, or with the help of market research companies.

You should ask them some of the same questions you asked your internal team during the interview and then compare their answers to your team's answers. How similar or different are the responses? Is there anything you overlooked or didn't realize? Does your approach or messaging need to be adjusted as a result?

Once you've tested your hypothesis, you're ready to use these insights to shape your marketing strategy and build your brand.

DESIGNING A MARKETING STRATEGY AROUND YOUR AUDIENCE

Start building your marketing strategies by creating buyer personas and then using these insights from the workshop to shape your overall approach to marketing. This helps you determine the areas of key interest, the messages your audience needs to hear, and how you'll deliver your messaging to them. It allows you to focus on and adopt almost an ABM approach to build relationships at scale and really support the sales team in their efforts.

Once you have your buyer personas, consider how these insights can be implemented on a more tactical level. After all, your strategy is only as good as its execution.

Fish Where the Fish Are: Identifying the Best Channels

One key question to ask when creating buyer personas is, "Where does your audience spend their time online?"

Knowing this information allows you to get in front of them on channels and platforms they already use before you have brand awareness. This will make it easier to reach them where they are, or as I like to say, "Fish where the fish are." After all, it's highly unlikely that your audience will wake up and visit your website, but they will wake up and go to their preferred social media channel.

Identifying the places your audience already frequents also allows you to be more effective and strategic with your efforts. By being more specific, you can avoid the scattergun approach and zero in on activities that will give you the best results. For example, instead of being on all social media channels, you can focus on the channels where they're most active—like LinkedIn for B2B marketers—or focus on specific publications, media outlets, and communities that cater specifically to your audience.

We've used this technique at CopyHouse to decide which communities we'd join. Rather than joining associations with a high concentration of agencies, we've focused on associations and communities with brands and CMOs (our target audience). This has allowed us to be more strategic and ensure our time and money are spent building relationships with our ideal buyer personas instead of barking up the wrong tree.

Identifying the Type of Content

After you've identified your primary channels, you then need to decide on the type of content. Content should be aligned with your audience's pain points and needs to ensure it delivers real value by helping them solve a challenge.

Since each persona has different challenges, you'll need different types of content and maybe even different mediums. For example, a busy CMO may engage better with video or podcasts than written content, while a CFO might like more granular details and want thought-leadership e-books.

When you understand your audience, you'll understand the type of content they'll find most beneficial and meaningful. You'll also understand their online behaviors, so not only where they already spend their time but what keywords they might use, whom they might follow, and what time they're most likely to be active online.

All your marketing efforts should come back to whom you're trying to speak with. I find it's easiest to incorporate this from the very beginning rather than trying to reverse-engineer campaigns. To do this, I assign buyer personas to each piece of content in a content calendar. Who's the audience for that social post, e-book, blog, event, or podcast?

Staying focused on the audience from the get-go makes it much easier to stay on brand and on track when designing campaigns and creating content.

Crafting Your Message

"If you could have a direct conversation with your audience, what would they need/want to know?"

When you're drafting your content, think about who you're speaking with and envision you're having a direct, one-to-one conversation. I'll sometimes imagine them sitting on the other side of the keyboard. You're not writing to the world; you're writing to that specific person.

If you were speaking with them, who would they be? What would they look like? What would you want them to know? What concerns would they have, and how can you ease them? What would you want to tell them?

Marketing, especially content marketing, is all about having conversations. But unlike direct physical conversations, marketing allows you to have these conversations at scale so you can grow a community and support your sales team. It would be almost impossible to have the same number of in-person conversations as you can have with marketing, which is why many companies without dedicated marketing efforts rely overly on outbound sales and heavily staffed SDR teams. The man-hours required for scaling relationships and supporting buyers are nearly impossible without marketing.

But done effectively, marketing, especially marketing attuned to buyer personas' worries, pain points, and needs, allows you to create relationships at scale and supercharge sales teams' efforts.

Chapter 3

Marketing vs. Sales: Investing in Your Marketing

Before a company starts investing in its marketing, it will probably rely on big SDR teams or external sales agencies to bring in leads. Without brand awareness, it's nearly impossible to create demand or generate inbound inquiries. Instead, sales teams are expected to use more traditional techniques, like knocking on doors, and are almost expected to "magic up" or produce leads from thin air as they don't have inbound leads to work from.

This approach almost never works as sales teams struggle to produce results. Either they or the business owner then gets frustrated, and after about 18 months, on average, the SDR will either leave or be let go. It's not really the businesses or SDR's fault, but this frustrating situation is a byproduct of not having strong marketing efforts.

I made this mistake in the early days of CopyHouse. I wanted to increase our sales volume, and naturally thought it was logical to hire an external sales consultant. At the time, we had almost no marketing efforts so we had no brand awareness, and we certainly weren't generating any inbound leads.

The sales consultant had decades of experience with agencies, so I thought they'd be able to help us, too. While they were able to help me identify some of the sales collateral we needed, like a proper pitch deck, they struggled to generate leads. Using traditional techniques like cold calling and outbound emails, they achieved no results. I wasted a few thousand dollars (which was a significant amount for us at the time), and after a few months, I had no alternative but to part ways with them.

I thought that our problem, like many businesses, was sales. After all, it was more sales we needed. But sales are not a sales problem—it's a marketing problem. Sales don't magically come from nowhere; they come from consistent marketing. As someone who runs a marketing agency, I should have realized this and begun our journey by investing in marketing before sales. To achieve the best results, sales teams need marketing teams to create leads, build opportunities for connections, and help streamline the buying experience. Sales can't work in isolation.

Think of it as a rugby team. Marketers are the forwards who fight for the ball (or leads) and then pass it to the sales teams, who then run it down the field and score. You need both parts of the team to win the game. Having only one side is almost useless.

If you're serious about your company's growth, you need to properly invest in marketing. That means treating it as a separate function from sales and creating the right resources, both internal teams and a dedicated budget.

The Problem with Sales and Marketing

I often see companies make one of three mistakes: sales run the show with marketing reporting into sales and only receiving a portion of their budget, overly investing in sales or outbound marketing, or making marketing and sales separate to the point that they are working in silos. While silos tend to be more common in larger organizations, both situations are extremely problematic as they don't create a healthy environment for growth or brand building.

Marketing Reports to Sales

I often meet marketing managers who are frustrated and upset because they need to report to and share their budget with sales. This often happens when sales are still seen as the driving force in the organization, which often happens if the company hasn't truly bought into investing in marketing.

Frequently, there's a fear or hesitation to invest fully in marketing as it's seen as an unknown quantity. As a result, this situation is quite common in technology companies with more introverted founders who come from a technical background. They want the results to be predicted ahead of time so (you spend X, and you'll receive Y), but as almost all marketers know, forecasting is often difficult, if not impossible.

While this might not seem problematic, it causes marketing and brand-building activities to be focused almost exclusively on bottom-of-funnel activities or events. Sales teams operate very differently from marketing and are often under pressure to meet monthly or quarterly sales targets. As a result, their activities focus on things like attending conferences, cold calling, outbound emails, or paid advertising like PPC. It's good to have these in the mix, but by focusing almost entirely on these activities, companies miss out on top or mid-funnel activities, which are essential for organic growth and creating brand awareness—a key ingredient for producing a consistent, steady stream of leads.

Sales Over Marketing

Another common mistake I see is companies that invest heavily in sales efforts but neglect marketing. Often, especially if the company has not invested in marketing, this can initially be out of necessity as it's the only way to produce any opportunities. However, these opportunities are often low quality and are unlikely to convert as the touchpoints don't exist to nurture leads through the pipeline.

For example, one of my consulting clients had been working with an outbound sales agency. They hadn't done any marketing and were relying almost exclusively on this agency to create leads. Over the course of a year, they spent nearly $60,000, and by the time I became involved, they were yet to win any new clients. Sure, the agency could create interesting conversations with relevant brands, but these conversations often didn't go past the initial meeting and were soon forgotten. Not having marketing efforts meant that there was no way to keep the conversations going with invites to events, staying top of mind with social media content, and newsletters or interviews for thought leadership content.

I also see this situation with internal hires. A company might have a six-person-strong sales team with SDRs and a chief growth officer who has a dedicated budget and spends a lot of time going to conferences and events. The same company might either not have anyone in a marketing role or have only one marketing manager who has to fight the sales team for budget or protect their budget from being eaten by the sales team. When there are six against one, marketing hardly stands a chance.

Instead, marketing should be seen as an equal investment. Similar to how you might put money into your savings account and investment portfolio each month, you want to invest in *both* sales and marketing and avoid overcompensating or relying on one rather than the other.

Marketing and Sales Don't Speak

Sometimes, sales and marketing teams fall into the habit of not communicating with each other and working in silos. When marketing and sales work in silos, it creates situations where the right hand doesn't know what the left hand is doing, and efforts aren't as efficient or successful as they should be.

For example, the marketing team may run a really successful campaign that generates lots of inbound leads but then the sales team doesn't pick up or follow up on these leads. There are no further conversations, and these initial leads fade into memory. Senior marketers are left scratching their heads and, quite unfairly, get the blame as the company sometimes starts to think that marketing doesn't work.

Marketing does indeed work, but it needs a good relationship with the sales team, including the right processes between departments, to be successful. Breaking down silos can seem overwhelming at first, especially within large organizations with complex office politics, but achieving better coordination between sales and marketing can be a game-changer.

Start by establishing clear lines of communication and sharing plans between departments and at the very least, having regular calls between sales and marketing to sync on activities and share strategies. What marketing campaigns are coming up? What activities can marketing support with? Creating open discourse is the first step toward building a better relationship.

CREATING HARMONY BETWEEN SALES AND MARKETING

Untangling problems within existing sales and marketing teams or decreasing your reliance on outbound sales to redirect investment into marketing can seem complicated or unnerving at first. While getting the right balance between sales and marketing may not be easy, doing so is essential for truly unlocking growth and creating a brand that consistently produces leads and grows revenue.

When I started CopyHouse, I didn't have a single contact to my name as I didn't come from an agency background and didn't have a little black book. Every opportunity needed to be created from scratch, and I had to build the brand from the ground up. I've always contributed our success to getting the right balance between sales and marketing and investing in our marketing early. Getting our approach right has allowed me to grow the company from zero in sales to $1 million in two years and $1.5 million by year four—an impressive feat considering most agencies don't make the million mark.

I don't share this to brag but to showcase the power of investing in marketing and creating harmony between sales and marketing.

Marketing Before Sales

When you want to grow revenue, it's natural to think that you need more salespeople. But this only works if you've already invested in your marketing. Marketing creates the leads, and sales bring the leads home and turn them into paying customers. So, you need to invest in marketing *before* you invest in sales.

After parting ways with the external sales consultant, I realized that my approach had been wrong. I needed to invest in marketing to build a community around us but also to give us a way to interact with potential clients without going directly for the hard sell. So, I hired a marketing manager, gave them a dedicated budget, and really began our journey of investing in our marketing. This set the foundation for the rapid growth we experienced during the pandemic and was perhaps one of the smartest decisions I've made when growing CopyHouse.

In regard to timelines, ideally, you should begin investing in marketing at least six months before hiring a salesperson. Creating organic momentum takes an average of six months before it will produce results, so investing in marketing *before* sales gives you enough time to start seeing the benefit of marketing and makes your sales team's jobs significantly easier.

Leveling the Playing Field

If you already have a sales and marketing team, it may be a matter of untangling the wires and creating a level playing field—rather than building one from scratch.

Start by creating a clear marketing budget and balancing the number of individuals on each team. If you have a five-person SDR team, rather than hiring more salespeople, consider bolstering the marketing team to allow them to achieve more and ultimately create more leads to feed the sales team. You'll probably find that by investing more in marketing, you can decrease your reliance on outbound sales agencies or hefty sales teams. Similarly, if you have a shared budget between marketing and sales, create a separate budget for each. Marketing and sales should be treated as equally important parts of growing your brand.

Untangling these wires will ease a lot of the frustrations within the teams and give them both a chance to really succeed. I've met far too many marketing managers who are at their wit's end. They're expected to do it all as a one-person team but aren't being given the tools or budget to do their job properly and are constantly at odds with the sales team. This situation not only hurts your overall marketing efforts and makes it much harder to build brand awareness but also leads to high churn rates within the marketing team as they'll eventually seek employment elsewhere.

Defining Lead Nurturing Processes

Once your marketing is up and running, you should start receiving inbound leads. But what happens after those leads are created?

Most companies, especially B2B companies, have long sales pipelines, with the average B2B sale taking between six to twelve months—if not longer. So, it's essential to think about how these leads are nurtured throughout the funnel and identify ways to streamline this process. Are there parts of the funnel that experience a high drop-out rate or where customers get stuck? How can you help them overcome these hurdles and be ready to convert sooner?

Mapping the customer journey is perhaps one of the best ways to unite sales and marketing, as it requires departments to collaborate and take shared responsibility for a streamlined customer journey. Marketing is responsible for creating the right touchpoints at the right time, while sales are responsible for understanding the best timing for these touchpoints and ensuring they're used strategically; for example, ensuring the right prospects are invited to an invite-only roundtable or reaching out to prospects who have downloaded the e-book.

You'll also be missing a trick if you haven't done this exercise before and don't have a good understanding of your customer journey, as your current customer journey is probably longer and messier than it needs to be. You might not realize when or where you're losing prospects and certainly won't be creating opportunities to keep them engaged. Taking a strategic approach to your customer journey allows you to address these challenges and ensure sales and marketing are working from the same page so you can shorten sales cycles and reach your growth goals sooner.

Creating a Marketing Strategy Aligned with the Sales Team

Your marketing strategy should work to feed and support your sales team. What activities are they planning? How can we make sure we get the most out of these opportunities by having dedicated marketing campaigns?

I often recommend that marketing teams divide their marketing efforts so they have standard business-as-usual activities on social, blog content, and events that serve to raise brand awareness and then create dedicated campaigns that support the sales team's efforts.

When creating the strategy for ongoing marketing requirements, it's often helpful to think about the type of content that might support your sales team and, as we explored previously, help streamline the customer journey. To align with the sales team, you might think about the type of information your audience needs to know before speaking to someone in your sales team. Can we make this information more accessible, for example, by featuring it on the website so they don't need to have a call to answer their initial questions? Once they do have a call, what are the most common questions or concerns your sales team hears from prospects? What collateral would help them address these concerns?

Thinking strategically about the type of information your prospects need allows you to ensure your marketing efforts work with your sales efforts and that the business-as-usual content is as beneficial to your audience as possible. Of course, not all content will be sales-focused, and neither should it be, but you also want to ensure your prospects can find the information they need when they need it.

For campaign-focused marketing, these campaigns might be led by your sales team's activities or vice versa. For example, if your company is speaking at a conference, what content can be produced around the conference to get the most from the event? Can a QR code for a downloadable e-book be shared on the last slide of the talk to capture leads? Can you create on-the-ground social media content? Conversely, how can your sales team support your marketing efforts? If you have an upcoming event, can they invite prospects or share the e-book you've created as a way to kick-start conversations?

CREATING A DEDICATED MARKETING BUDGET

Given the importance of marketing in creating leads and supporting the sales team, I'm always surprised that companies don't create a dedicated marketing budget. Either that budget is shared with the sales team or, perhaps even worse, not defined at all and left entirely up to chance.

I won't work with a consulting client that hasn't identified a marketing budget. As a consultant, my job is to create a marketing strategy, which is impossible without a budget and knowing how much you can spend. The marketing budget determines how much can be accomplished and how quickly. It influences the approach you take. Depending on the budget, you'll be able to determine whether it's reasonable and realistic to go after multiple buyer personas, geographies, and industries or if you'll need to be more selective. It also determines if you can compete directly with large, well-funded brands or if you'll need to take a scrappier approach.

Since the budget is such a determining factor in your approach, you need to set the budget *before* you create the strategy. After all, without a budget, there's not much point in even having a strategy, as you won't be able to implement it.

Overcoming Initial Hesitations

I think many brands don't set marketing budgets, not because they don't want to but because they're unsure how much they should be spending and aren't assured of the results. It's notoriously difficult to track and prove the value of marketing, as a lot of the value comes from relationship-building activities and may not pay dividends for months. More risk-averse roles, like the CFO—who tends to be in control of determining the budget—are, as a result, hesitant. They worry about investing in marketing without clearly defined results. If the value of marketing isn't fully explained to them, then it's much harder, if not impossible, to secure a budget.

One of the best ways to overcome this hesitation is by helping them see the bigger picture and the role marketing plays in the future of the company. Marketing activities, especially those at the top and mid-funnel, may not deliver a return for six to twelve months, depending on the company's sales cycles. It can also be helpful to explain the cost of *not* investing in marketing like continuing to rely on expensive outbound approaches or losing market share to competitors. The fear of loss can be a powerful motivator, especially for risk-averse individuals.

Determining the Budget

How much should you spend on your marketing activities? It's an age-old question.

While there's no hard and fast rule, I often recommend that brands start by investing 5 to 10 percent of their overall turnover in marketing. You should then update this amount quarterly. Within this range, you typically need to spend at least 5 percent to maintain market position and hold your position against competitors who'll be investing at least this amount. Otherwise, you risk moving backward and losing market share as customers build brand affinity and relationships with more well-known brands.

If you spend less than 5 percent, your company will be in real trouble. So much so that I tell our marketing manager off if she's not spending enough and ensuring our marketing budget is going toward building our brand. Having a budget that isn't used doesn't help anyone. Indeed, an unspent budget often gets reabsorbed into the company, so it never contributes to building the brand.

If you have ambitious growth goals, you should spend closer to 10 percent. This allows you to invest enough to grow your share of voice and attract new customers to the brand. It also allows you to match and exceed competitors' efforts and should give your marketing team enough support to fulfill marketing strategies and deliver tangible results. I typically steer our budget toward the middle of this range, with our budget set at 8 percent.

It's important to remember that 5 to 10 percent is a ballpark estimate that should work for most brands. If you want a more precise figure, consider your competitors, buyer personas, target markets/geographies, and overall business plans. These factors will impact how much you should spend and whether you need to spend more than ten percent.

Continue Investing During a Downturn

Over the last three years, we've witnessed a global pandemic, conflict on the world stage, recessions, and large-scale redundancies. So naturally, most brands are considering their marketing investments and whether they should reduce the amount they spend. Marketers are expected to do more with less, as marketing budgets are often one of the first things to be cut when a company experiences difficulties.

I think cutting marketing budgets is a massive mistake. While I'm clearly biased, marketing activities are a long-term investment in brand equity and the company's future. So, while you may not see an impact of cutting marketing budgets today, it'll impact how quickly you can recover and grow post-market slump.

Research supports this viewpoint, as companies that increase their marketing spending during recessions often increase their sales by 20 percent over pre-recession levels, while those that cut marketing spending can expect to see a 7 percent decrease in sales. Companies that continue to invest, even during a market downturn, ensure their brands can survive and ultimately thrive.

I experienced this firsthand during the pandemic. While many agencies were cutting spending and furloughing team members, I didn't want to make the same cuts. So, I looked hard at what we did, identified our niche, and then used the government-backed bounce-back loan to invest in building our brand. Investing in our marketing allowed us to begin building a brand very early on and allowed us to slingshot out of the pandemic—setting much of the foundation for our growth.

I've seen similar results from our clients who continued to invest during market downturns, so I know the power of maintaining marketing spending and ensuring your company is standing—and thriving—post-downturn.

Hiring a Marketing Manager Is Different from Creating a Budget

Hiring a marketing manager is different from identifying and creating a budget. Many companies think that they can hire a marketing manager who can then carry out all activities with little (or sometimes no) budget. While this is a fairly common way of thinking, it's extremely problematic.

Marketing is such an extensive field that it would be nearly impossible for one marketing manager to be equally skilled across all areas. Furthermore, a good marketing strategy should feature a wide range of activities, which makes it nearly impossible for a marketing manager to execute.

Even if they could, some elements will simply require spending money. For example, even the best marketing manager can't print brochures or host a 12-person dinner with food, drinks, and venue without spending a penny. So, they'll need a budget, and this budget will help them determine the suppliers they can use and their overall approach and empower them to make decisions without constantly seeking sign-off. Without a budget, a marketing manager is like a dog without teeth.

Giving Your Marketing Investment Time

Investing in your marketing today is highly unlikely to impact your bottom line tomorrow. It takes consistent focus over time to build a brand and create real results.

However, one of the biggest challenges for brands, especially those investing in marketing for the first time, is being patient enough to start seeing the results. The first few months are magical: You're excited about the potential, but then you hit a slump around the six-month mark, where you start to feel impatient, uncomfortable, and fed up, as the results seem to have stalled. But push past this slump, and you start to see a real impact.

Achieving organic momentum takes time. I often explain that it's like building a snowball. You pack the snowball and push it down the hill, and as it gets going, it builds momentum until it's a massive snowball that moves at speed. Getting your marketing up and running is similar. You might not see results at first, or they might seem slow-moving, but as you continue to invest, you start to see a steady stream of inbound leads that prove that marketing *does* work.

You can typically work out the amount of time it'll take by looking at your time-to-close rate. How long does it currently take for a lead to become a client? Your time-to-close rate is typically the amount of time it'll take to see any impact on the bottom line, as any new activities or approaches will need to run through this process before you can see results. The worst thing you can do is switch approaches or pull the plug too soon, as you'll then lose any insights into whether it worked and waste the initial investment.

Chapter 4

Hiring a Marketing Manager and Creating Dedicated Resource

Once you have your marketing budget, you'll then need to think about how you use this budget and, perhaps, more importantly, who will use it. At this point, you'll probably think about hiring a marketing manager. I normally recommend that brands hire a marketing manager as soon as they're able, as having this role in the company really accelerates your ability to build brand awareness and successfully reach your growth goals.

WHY YOU NEED A MARKETING MANAGER

I meet many businesses that are resistant to hiring a marketing manager and try to hold off on hiring one. These businesses come in all shapes and sizes, and it's not only a challenge that startups and early-stage companies face. Normally, this hesitation stems from the fact that marketing is difficult to measure and doesn't have an immediate impact on revenue or the bottom line. Marketing is often classed as a non-billable role because it doesn't contribute to a sellable product or service. Marketing managers' time isn't billed to clients and they don't typically build products.

However, I think marketing managers have one of the most important roles in any company, as they create demand for your product or service. All companies need both supply and demand to harness fast-paced growth.

Without a marketing manager, it's nearly impossible to build a brand and, therefore, create demand. Strong brands attract the right customers, drive inbound leads (demand), and elevate your company profile. It's a full-time job (plus some) that really requires focused attention. Companies will sometimes ask other team members to take on this responsibility, but this rarely works.

Other team members, especially those outside of marketing, simply don't have the bandwidth to focus on marketing, often don't understand the strategic thinking required for effective marketing, and are easily pulled into other activities. Then, marketing doesn't happen or only happens in an ad-hoc, inconsistent manner, which makes it difficult to achieve traction.

I spend a lot of my time speaking with companies and can honestly say that I've never met a company with fast-paced growth that didn't have a dedicated marketing function. So, you'll inevitably need to hire a marketing manager. It's almost unavoidable.

THE PROBLEM WITH FOUNDER-LED MARKETING

Before a company hires a marketing manager, the founder or senior leadership team often attempts to run the marketing program, but I've never seen a company successfully make this *actually* work.

Most founders are entrepreneurial in spirit, which is why they started their companies in the first place, but this also means that they're easily distracted by new ideas and approaches (shiny object syndrome). They're also often involved in other areas of the business, which creates conflicting priorities, and these other areas can take center stage as the problems are more urgent or seen as more business-critical. Immediate problems take priority over more long-term activities, like marketing, and distract from building brand equity for the future of the company. As a result, companies are left living very much in the moment and often living hand to mouth as they go through constant feast-to-famine cycles.

When things are busy, founders struggle to find time for marketing and, therefore, only focus on marketing when things are slower. This inconsistency creates a feast-to-famine situation. The only way to escape the feast-to-famine cycle is with consistent marketing efforts, which is why hiring a marketing manager is so important.

Furthermore, founders are often far too close to the forest to see the trees and can struggle to take an objective view of their company—there's no such thing as an ugly baby. Without this objective view, it's difficult to see the brand from the customers' point of view and create marketing that actually resonates with the audience. By being too close to the forest, founders can also easily view marketing as a cost rather than an investment, which makes it difficult to create a marketing budget or give marketing managers the power they need to make decisions quickly.

Hiring a marketing manager can help overcome many of these challenges and is an essential part of growing the company. It allows founders to move away from marketing and focus on activities required for growing the company—like defining the company's future vision or securing funding from investors. By moving away from marketing, founders can empower their marketing teams to move at speed and build a brand that connects internal experts with their audience in a way their audience will understand.

Escaping the Cobbler's Shoes Dilemma

Before hiring a marketing manager, companies sometimes attempt to deliver marketing campaigns by using existing team members whose primary role isn't marketing. This is particularly common when the subject-matter experts aren't part of the marketing team, are senior leaders or specialists in other areas of the business, or when creative skills exist outside of marketing, like within digital marketing agencies.

However, this approach almost never works, as these team members have other responsibilities that are part of their day jobs and almost inevitably have conflicts or more immediate priorities that relegate marketing to the back burner. Without designated responsibility, marketing just doesn't happen.

It's an easy mistake to make and one that I'm guilty of. I used to think that our copywriters could write content for the CopyHouse blog. Of course, our copywriters had the skills to write our marketing content but almost never had the time. Every week for an entire year, I asked them to create an article, and without fail, a more immediate client requirement came in and the article got pushed back to the following week. This vicious cycle continued for almost an entire year until I finally realized that despite having the skill sets within the team, we needed dedicated resources to consistently be able to create content for our own marketing efforts.

Strong processes can help overcome this challenge to a degree. We have since developed processes and systems for prioritizing work that allow us to create content on occasion internally. However, even with these processes, conflicting demands often mean that marketing is a low priority. It's difficult to make a paying client wait so we can create our own marketing, and it is much easier to rely on external support to achieve our marketing aims and avoid falling into the very classic cobbler's shoe trap.

While relying on team members with creative skill sets is probably more common with marketing agencies, I've also come across this problem in tech companies, but normally for different reasons.

Almost all tech companies have very brilliant people who work there, people who know their area of expertise extremely well, have spent decades perfecting their knowledge and should be thought leaders. I'm always amazed by the level of expertise within tech companies, especially within very niche areas. While tapping into this expertise is definitely the right approach, asking subject-matter experts to actually create the content rarely is.

Subject-matter experts are not marketers and are often over-stretched already, so they struggle to consistently produce content. Having them create content often isn't a good or cost-effective use of their time. If they'll need to spend five to ten hours writing an e-book, this is not only costly given their high salaries but also takes away from their ability to build the product, service customers, or lead the business. Even if they can find the time to create content, this content is often very technical and doesn't speak to the audience in a way they understand. Since the subject-matter experts know the topics so well, they easily fall into the information gap and assume everyone understands to the same degree that they do. But, of course, this isn't correct as your clients wouldn't need you if they understood to the same degree.

So, while it can be tempting to rely on existing team members for their creative skill sets or expertise, this often doesn't produce the best marketing results. The only way to overcome the cobbler shoe syndrome and achieve consistent, customer-centric marketing is by having dedicated marketing resources—normally a full-time marketing manager.

Protecting Marketing Resources

Once you've hired a marketing manager, it's important to protect this resource and ensure they don't get pulled into projects outside of marketing or stray off course.

A marketing manager should be 110 percent focused on building your company's brand and shouldn't get involved with projects outside of this realm. Client projects or product builds can eat up quite a lot of their time and become a bit of a slippery slope. Once they start becoming involved in other projects, their time quickly becomes consumed with work that doesn't contribute to implementing marketing campaigns and creating long-term value by building your brand.

I've always been quite protective of our marketing manager's time. While it's occasionally been tempting to have them help the team on client projects, especially if we have tight deadlines or other team members are out sick, creating pressure on resources, I've also realized the importance of protecting their time. It can be difficult as not everyone in the company understands, and occasionally, there are conflicts around how their time is best spent. However, by taking a firm stance from the beginning, it becomes much easier to manage expectations and keep this option off the table.

Larger organizations may not have the same temptation to use marketing in client projects but face another challenge in protecting marketing managers' time. For larger organizations, this often happens in the form of endless meetings. Marketing impacts all areas of the business, so it's easy to think that marketing team members should be present at all internal meetings. But back-to-back meetings take away from the time they have for delivering marketing activities and ultimately distract from actually building your brand. As a result, it's important to be selective over the meetings marketing managers attend and ensure they have enough time to deliver campaigns.

HIRING THE RIGHT MARKETING MANAGER

I decided to hire a marketing manager very early in building CopyHouse. We hired our first marketing manager as our fifth position only six months after launching the company, which was extremely early compared to most agencies. However, I believe that hiring a marketing manager helped accelerate our growth as we were able to focus and dedicate resources toward building the brand from the very beginning and ensuring we set the right foundations. I think it's perhaps one of the smartest decisions I've made while building CopyHouse.

However, I also know firsthand how difficult it can be to actually find the right person for the role. It's not an easy hire as you need a specific person with a specific skill set at the right time in their career and from the right background to really succeed. Since hiring our first marketing manager, we've needed to replace this individual three separate times, and each hire has taught me some valuable lessons about how to hire a marketing manager.

I now help our consulting clients find the right marketing manager and know exactly what I'm looking for when making this hire. By being very specific as to requirements, it's much easier to move away from long hiring cycles with multiple interviews with different stakeholders and unpaid tasks and avoid making the wrong hire. Hiring the wrong marketing manager could massively set you back or send you down the wrong road, wasting your time and money barking up the wrong tree.

Determining the Right Skill Level

Before you can hire a marketing manager, it's important to understand the skill level you're looking for. Most companies fall into one of two traps when hiring their first marketing manager. They either hire someone far too senior by wanting to hire the very best or hire someone far too junior without thinking about the support these more junior employees need. In actuality, the ideal solution lies somewhere between as most companies should look to hire a mid-level marketing manager.

Senior Marketing Managers

It can be tempting to hire a very experienced marketing manager, marketing director, or CMO as your first marketing hire. I think it's especially easy to make this mistake if you don't know much about marketing, as you naturally want someone who knows more about you. Companies that understand the importance of marketing are probably also more likely to make this mistake as they want to invest in their marketing by hiring the very best talent possible.

However, the more senior a marketing manager is, the less likely they are to roll up their sleeves and get involved in the actual delivery. Instead, they will want to focus on the marketing strategy and big-picture thinking. While you'll need some degree of strategic thinking, you'll also want someone who isn't so senior that they don't want to get involved in the implementation.

I made this mistake with our very first hire and hired someone who was far too experienced. I was impressed by their background and flattered that they wanted to be part of CopyHouse. Having someone with decades of experience seemed like a very good idea. However, I soon learned that this was not actually the case. While she did have some good experience, she was at the point in her career where they wanted to focus on the strategy, wanted a larger budget than we could provide, and eventually got frustrated and left. Building a brand from scratch is very different from continuing the momentum of an existing brand, something *most* senior marketing managers with impressive resumes aren't familiar with. Just because they have an impressive background or have worked with notable brands doesn't mean that they're the right fit for you.

Junior Marketing Execs

I also see companies go to another extreme by hiring a very junior marketing executive or recent graduate and then expecting them to deliver the same level of output as a more senior marketing manager. Most junior marketing executives or recent grads don't have enough experience to fully deliver in this role, and the company, likewise, doesn't have enough bandwidth or resources to support them fully—a lose-lose situation.

Typically, companies make this mistake when they don't fully understand the value of marketing, are hesitant to add a higher salary to their payroll, or are trying to keep costs low. They've often been told by investors or peers that they *should* invest in marketing but are making their first forays and, as such, don't quite know the best approach.

While hiring a junior marketing executive may seem like a good idea, it often backfires. More junior hires require a lot of support from more senior team members, distracting them from their roles. Junior marketing executives may have lower salaries, but they require far more handholding and take longer to get up and running before they can deliver the expected results. Hiring a junior marketing executive can make building a brand a more tedious and certainly less effective process.

You'll also need to consider how and who might support them, especially if they're your first marketing hire. Do you have someone on the team with marketing experience who can teach them the ropes and help them learn the skills of the trade? Who will they turn to when they have questions or need guidance? Suppose you don't already have a marketing team. In that case, it's unlikely that you'll be able to deliver the right level of support, and not having this support system in place can be quite traumatic for individuals in the early stages of their careers.

I've met quite a few marketing managers who are scared by these early career experiences. Often, they were hired at companies without marketing functions and were expected to deliver the same level of results as seasoned marketing professionals without having the skills or budget to do so. Feeling like you can't deliver, even when it's not entirely your fault, has a big impact on confidence levels and can leave them with baggage for many years to come.

Mid-Level Marketing Managers

In my opinion, mid-level marketing managers offer the perfect middle ground. Someone with four to five years of marketing experience offers the ideal mix by being junior enough to want to roll up their sleeves and implement marketing campaigns while also being experienced enough to work independently and have a degree of strategic thinking.

I also typically look for someone who can grow into the role. You want to take a long-term view with this hire as, ideally, they'll stay at the company for at least two years. Marketing takes time to implement, so you want to hire someone who has the potential to last. You don't want someone who will get bored quickly as they've already mastered many of the skills and will soon be looking for their next role. As a result, you want to look for someone with the right skills but also someone who shows potential and an appetite for learning. Typically, this is someone with a few years of experience but is looking for their next step up by moving into their first marketing manager role or second marketing manager role within a larger company.

Finding the Right Skill Set

I meet with many companies that expect their marketing manager to do everything and be able to deliver all elements of a marketing strategy without additional support. The expectation that they can do everything is perhaps one of the biggest problems for marketing managers.

Marketing covers extensive ground, so much so that it's almost impossible for one person to be equally good in all areas. One marketing campaign could easily cover disciplines as different as paid advertising, event management, copywriting, design and so much more. Expecting that your marketing manager can execute all these elements is far from reasonable.

When finding someone with the right skill set, there are two main approaches—either hiring a generalist with experience across the disciplines or hiring a marketing manager with a strong skill set in a specific area with the idea that they will then work alongside an agency, freelancer, or other team member to deliver the campaign.

Generalist marketing managers should be responsible for overseeing the larger strategy and bringing in the right resources to deliver the campaign. They should have enough experience across the disciplines to manage partners, freelancers, or interns but are unlikely to be experts in one particular area. After all, if you need a full-time expert in copywriting, you're better off hiring a copywriter.

Think of it like this: You're about to embark on the journey, and your marketing manager should be seen as the driver of the van. They're in charge of the direction of travel, navigating the roads, and identifying the people they need to help them reach the final destination.

They can't do the drive alone but need people to help them on the journey. These people might be a network of partners, marketing team members, freelancers, etc.

Alternatively, you can also hire a marketing manager with a strong skill set in your main area of focus. For example, if your marketing strategy is focused on building communities via live events, hiring a marketing manager with event management experience could be a good idea. However, to leverage this approach, you'll need to already have a good understanding of your marketing strategy *before* hiring so you can identify the right person. Working with a fractional CMO can be a good idea as they can define your strategy and then help you hire someone with the relevant skills. You'll then need to supplement any areas they're weak in with external partners or additional hires. This allows them to work with people who have complementary skills and can build a team.

I've used both approaches when hiring a marketing manager at CopyHouse. We hired a generalist marketing manager as our second hire to help us define the strategy while also implementing some of the campaigns, but more recently, we hired a specialist marketing manager with a strong background in events, as we knew this would be the main focus of our strategy. The generalist approach works best for a first hire as you often don't know what will work with your audience and where you'll get the most traction. As your strategy develops, you'll identify key areas of focus and then be able to hire a more specialist marketing manager who can champion specific elements of marketing—like event management and community building.

Finding the Right Background: Startup vs. Corporate

When hiring a marketing manager, it's extremely important to consider their background in regards to the type of organization they've previously worked for and whether it'll be suitable for your company. You ideally want someone who comes from a similar environment and will be able to hit the ground running. It can be tempting to want to hire a marketing manager from a well-known brand, but if you're a start-up or scale-up, this corporate experience often doesn't translate well.

Corporate environments are extremely different from scale-ups, start-ups, or agencies. In the corporate world, marketing managers spend a lot of time in meetings and navigating office politics. Decisions are made much more slowly, there are extensive processes for sign-off, and they'll often have a larger marketing team to rely on. It can also be easier to hide within corporate environments as accountability is treated differently, and most individuals don't have as big an impact as in startups, scale-ups, or agencies.

Start-ups, scale-ups, and agencies are often fast-paced environments with limited resources, ambitious goals, and high expectations. It takes a certain type of person to thrive and enjoy this environment, and it can come as a shock to someone not used to it. Start-ups aren't for everyone. If you're making your first marketing hire, finding someone who's used to this type of environment will help you set the foundation for success and drastically increase your chances of retaining them.

Building a Brand from Scratch vs. Working on an Existing Brand

Before you hire a marketing manager, it's also important to consider your brand's current stage. Are you building a brand from scratch? Are you looking to revamp a legacy brand? Elevate an existing brand? Or something in between?

The current state of your brand will influence the profile of your ideal hire, as you typically want to hire someone with relevant brand-building experience. Your marketing manager should have experience building a brand from your current position, so they're familiar with the right approaches and challenges. Working on an existing brand is very different from building a brand from scratch and requires different techniques, approaches, and even mentality.

Existing brands need a marketing manager who can continue their momentum. Often, there'll be previous campaigns from which to draw insights as to what's worked or hasn't, and they already have an audience to market to. In this situation, the marketing manager's role is to capitalize on the success and help elevate the brand even further. However, when you're building a brand from scratch, you need to get the plane off the ground, which takes significantly more work as you need to find the audience, define the brand positioning, and be comfortable with failure, as not all techniques will work. It requires experimentation to discover the techniques that work for your specific audience and patience as you grow the brand.

I often think of building a brand like climbing Everest. If you hire a guide who's only familiar with the last leg of the journey, it'll be difficult for you to overcome some of the early pitfalls and challenges. You might not know how far it is to base camp or how much gear to bring. However, a guide who knows the entire route and has traveled that path before knows how to avoid these pitfalls, pack the right equipment, and ultimately get you safely to the top.

SUPPORTING YOUR MARKETING MANAGER

With most CMOs and marketing managers with 18 months of experience, it's essential to think about how you can support them and ensure they remain with the company long enough to implement your marketing strategy. It typically takes three to six months for them to fully get their feet under them and start producing results.

The short tenure in these positions is understandable as it can often be a lonely and isolating position, especially if they're the only marketing manager within the company. They won't necessarily have coworkers and teammates who understand the pressures of trying to deliver it all, being expected to produce leads from day one, and working within tight or limited budgets. Given that they may be the only ones with marketing expertise, they can also struggle to have a clear development plan as their line manager very likely won't know marketing well enough to identify where they can grow and develop. Without people to share their struggles with, they can often start to feel like their challenges are unique and become frustrated and disengaged.

However, it doesn't have to be this way, and I've spent a lot of my career building a community for marketing managers in this position. There are some very practical solutions for helping them feel connected and grow, even when they're a one-person team.

One practical way is to connect them with other marketing managers working at similar companies. Helping them meet others in similar positions within similar contexts allows them to share insights, solve challenges, and even strike up potential collaborations. I make sure our marketing manager knows other marketing managers at agencies and can create friendships. I also host my podcast "Tech Marketers Uncorked" and run a number of events in London and the US as a way to bring marketers together, help them learn new skills, and make the world feel a bit smaller.

I also invest in their training and development. One good way to identify skill gaps is by looking at the companies' wider business strategy, how this connects to the marketing strategy, and what skills are required to produce the best results. What marketing efforts have gone well? What areas are being overlooked or not invested in? Do you want to invest in these activities? How can you level up your marketing, and does your marketing manager need new skills to do so?

For example, we ran a really successful suite of live in-person events last year and really found our rhythm with in-person events. But we ran all of these events without partners or sponsors so one of our areas of focus this year is to increase partnerships. Given that it's a new area for our marketing manager, they'll likely require some support and training to make the most of these opportunities.

It is essential to ensure that your marketing manager feels supported, is surrounded by like-minded individuals who share their challenges, and has opportunities to grow. You don't want to hire a new marketing manager every few months, and you need them to stay in the position long enough to implement your marketing plan and start to see healthy traction.

Chapter 5

Creating a Website that Reflects Your Business

Your website is the foundation for everything you do, so it's essential to ensure it's in a good place before you start building your brand.

When running marketing campaigns, whether online or offline, all activity will eventually send people to your website. You might meet a prospect at a conference, someone might refer them to your business, or they might see your social media content, but regardless of how they hear about your business, at some point, they'll visit your website to learn more and decide whether you can be trusted to solve their problem.

When they visit your site, they want to know, relatively quickly, whether you can be trusted and if you have the expertise to address their needs. If your website is confusing, unclear, or overcomplicated, you'll lose trust and, effectively, sales. Your website needs help to put your best foot forward by clearly communicating your offerings and showing that you understand your audience.

Without a strong website, your marketing investment won't return the results it should, and the stronger your website, the stronger your overall results. Your website is the foundation for everything you do, and as such, it should be your number one priority when building your brand.

However, getting your website in a good place is no easy feat. It often takes a lot of time, energy, and resources to create a strong website. It should be treated as an ongoing investment rather than something that's done once and then left to rot.

NOT A ONE AND DONE

Think of your website as a constantly evolving organism. As your company grows and changes, your site should also grow and evolve so it can stay up to date with your company and reflect where you are now and in the future. Keeping your website aligned requires continual efforts and is something that should be reviewed regularly.

Once the main landing pages are in a good place (i.e., they reflect where you are and your current offerings), you can then shift your focus to areas like case studies or blog articles. Long-form content allows you to showcase your expertise and grow your digital presence by ranking for new keywords and appearing in search results. Every new blog article helps to increase your reach, increase organic traffic through SEO, and create new conversations with your audience. Regularly adding content to your website helps you increase your domain authority and digital prowess.

Think of your website as digital land. The more land you have, the greater your power and position. The king has the most land, so he has the most power. To dominate in your industry, you'll want to increase your kingdom and grow your website by adding new content.

I often come across companies that don't invest enough in their websites or, even worse, have created a website years (sometimes decades) ago and then left it. They mistakenly think that because they've created a website, it then doesn't need to be maintained or nurtured. I think this situation is particularly common with B2B companies that don't sell physical goods or services via their websites. Since they're not actively producing revenue or contributing to the bottom line, B2B websites are often seen as digital brochures. Their main objective is to provide information and hopefully encourage visitors to contact the sales team for a demo or discovery call so they aren't taken as seriously. However, even B2B companies need to continually invest and develop their websites to ensure they can put their best foot forward, send the right messages to their audience, and ensure their marketing activities, happening elsewhere, produce the best value.

CREATING YOUR WEBSITE

Before I start building a marketing strategy, one of the first questions I ask a new client is, "How do you feel about your website? Does it reflect who you are now and where you want to go?" How they answer these questions very quickly tells me whether we need to start by working on the website. I start here because the website will serve as the foundation for all future work and ensure my strategy can produce the best results.

You want a website that reflects where you are now and isn't outdated. Once you've brought your website up to speed, you can then think about using your website to position your company for your next stage of growth.

Now vs. Future

Positioning your website to reflect the "future" of your company is a good way to attract bigger clients or expand into a new market. However, striking the right balance to allow you to build credibility in a new market or with a new audience requires a special approach. You don't want to make your company appear to be something it's not.

If you're considering positioning your website for the future, it's helpful to start by thinking about where you want to go and, most importantly, *why*. Do you want to expand into a new market where you've seen credibility? Attract larger clients? Or do you want to start offering a new service or launching a new product?

If so, then work backward. What previous experiences do you have in these spaces? Have you worked with similar clients in that market (even if only on small projects)? Or do you want to draw on the company's history for launching a new product?

Once you have a clear direction, you can then think about how to bring this messaging to life. For example, suppose you've historically worked with smaller companies but want to pivot toward bigger brands. In that case, you might create case studies from the projects you've done with larger companies or feature their logos on your website. This showcases your expertise with bigger brands and helps you attract similar clients. Or if you're launching a new service line, you might have a dedicated landing page for that service with more general testimonies about working with you instead of client-specific case studies.

Both examples help to position you for a new stage of growth by building your expertise with a new audience or around a new service/product. It's important to think about how you want your website to represent your company before getting started.

Step 1: Getting Your Core Messaging Right

Your website is the only salesperson who can work 24/7 and be available around the clock to support your audience. It can be there on nights, weekends, and holidays when your human salespeople can't. So, it's essential to think about the messages it communicates and ensure you deliver the information your audience wants and needs at all times.

To achieve this, you need to start by identifying these key messages. You need to know the messages your audience needs to hear, what burning problems keep them awake and online at 2 a.m., and how you can support your audience before they speak to someone in your team. If you want to be able to communicate the right messages at the right time, you need to define your core messaging before you begin building your site.

Core messaging is essentially your brand identity in written form. Most of us are familiar with brand identity but from a visual perspective, such as logos, color palettes, typography, etc. Think of core messaging as the other half of this equation. It's all the key messages that capture your brand essence and everything that makes you unique.

Your core messaging shapes the overall direction of your website, including the landing pages you need, what keywords you should target, and what blog content or case studies you should produce. It's basically all the ingredients you need to create an effective website that speaks directly to your audience. Similar to baking a cake, you need to line up all your ingredients and make sure you have everything required before you begin.

Your core messaging should capture your positioning statement, your what, how, and why, and your target audience, including pain points and benefit-driven USPs. While there are many ways to create this messaging, it's often easiest to run a workshop with an external provider who can give perspective and help you see the forest from the trees.

The Case for Core Messaging

I went through this process before creating our first website. I had a team member run one of the workshops we use with clients and found it very therapeutic to dive into the messaging around the business, my aspirations for our growth, and how I wanted to communicate this to the world. Before doing this exercise, all the information was only in my head, which meant that our team didn't have the same information, and there wasn't consensus across the board. Capturing and documenting all of these insights made it significantly easier to create our first website. While this messaging has evolved over time, it's served as the backbone for all of our work as I could refer back to the messaging throughout our growth to ensure we were headed in the right direction.

On the flip side, I have also created websites without first setting the foundations by creating the core messaging, and I almost always end badly. Inevitably, the founders and C-suite get upset and frustrated as they struggle to communicate the insights they have in their heads or disagree about what messages should be on the website. Taking the time to create core messaging relieves a lot of these problems by getting all stakeholders involved early on and creating a brand identity that everyone can stand behind. Furthermore, this brand identity can then act as the foundation for all future work, including onboarding new employees and suppliers as well as creating any personalized content like brochures, pitch decks, etc.

Step 2: Defining Your SEO Strategy

After you have your core messaging, you can start to build an SEO strategy by conducting keyword research and identifying primary and secondary keywords. Ensuring your website is properly optimized is essential for driving organic traffic and ensuring it continues to be one of your best salespeople. As such, every landing page should have at least one keyword that isn't used on other landing pages and offers the right balance between search volume, difficulty, and search intent.

I occasionally meet B2B companies that think they don't need to optimize their website. Since they don't sell products through their website and don't need a high volume of leads, they see their site as a brochure site rather than a site and a place to send people to actually produce leads. However, this isn't strictly true, and I think not optimizing your site is a massive, missed opportunity.

Optimizing your website allows you to get your company in front of an audience that is looking for your service but doesn't know your brand. It allows you to tap into a prospect base that is actively in the buying stage, so it is essential for all companies across all industries. However, the keywords you choose and how you choose keywords are different in the B2B sector.

I started my career working at an SEO agency, spending a lot of time conducting keyword research for B2C brands. B2C brands rely extensively on SEO to compete with competitors and attract organic traffic to their product pages. When conducting keyword research for B2C brands, you're always looking for the largest search volume with the lowest keyword difficulty. After all, if you're selling shoes, you need to sell thousands of pairs of shoes to be successful, as these are sold at a relatively low price point.

B2B is drastically different as you're not necessarily looking for quantity but quality. Your sales team doesn't need thousands of leads and probably couldn't handle thousands of leads every month, especially if they're using a more consultative sales approach. Instead, they need a handful of high-quality leads and securing one new large client a year could be a massive victory—depending on the size of the deal. As a result, SEO is very different in the B2B world as it becomes far more about search intent and less about search volume.

I was taught by an SEO agency that you would never optimize a landing page for a keyword with less than 1,000 search volume. However, very few B2B brands will have relevant keywords with as high a search volume without targeting very generic and not very relevant (fat head) keywords. Instead, most B2B brands are better targeting extremely relevant keywords; for example, I once created a website for a company that sold semiconductor parts and as you can imagine, the keywords didn't have high volumes. If I remember correctly, the keyword we chose, "semiconductor parts," had only 10 searches per month but a very low keyword difficulty as few brands were competing for this keyword, which meant that by targeting it, they could secure one to two inbound inquiries per month, which could result in over a million dollars in revenue. B2C companies would need to sell thousands of pairs of shoes to reach the same level of turnover.

I think B2B companies often, mistakenly, think SEO isn't relevant for them as they're only viewing it from the B2C perspective, where search volume reigns supreme. However, if you view SEO at its basic definition of positioning you in front of an audience who needs your service but doesn't know your brand, then it becomes far more relevant. I really believe that SEO is important for all brands, but you need to understand the right approaches and techniques based on business commercial elements to leverage correctly.

Creating an SEO Strategy for Your Website

I often recommend creating your SEO strategy after creating your core messaging and before writing the copy for your landing pages.

SEO data can tell you a lot about your audience, what they're looking for, and how you can align your website to cater to these needs. It's easiest to ensure your website is optimized for SEO by baking it in from the beginning.

I start by conducting keyword research to look for relevant keywords that have enough search volume without being overly difficult (especially for brands without massive budgets). Keyword difficulty tells you how hard a keyword will be to rank and, as a result, how many resources will need to be dedicated to securing a ranking on page 1. Ranking anywhere else is almost irrelevant, as no one goes past page 1.

I also look at any keyword rankings the brand might have. Since most companies have a website (even if their past website wasn't great), they'll naturally have some rankings, but often these rankings are on page 2 or lower. Optimizing landing pages around these keywords is often low-hanging fruit as it can quickly boost a brand to page 1.

Once I have a list of target keywords, I then map primary and secondary keywords for every landing page. Every landing page should have a keyword with the highest search volume without being overly difficult and while remaining very relevant to the information on the page. It's a fine balance that takes some practice but becomes easier and more intuitive as you go.

Step 3: Creating Landing Pages

Your core messaging and SEO strategy will determine the landing pages you create. Core messaging tells you the messages your audience needs to hear, while your SEO strategy justifies whether *enough* people are interested in creating a dedicated landing page. SEO also verifies whether your audience uses the same terms to search for your services as you use internally to talk about your product or services. Sometimes, there's a discrepancy between the terms a company uses internally and those used within the market.

Information Architecture: Parent & Child Pages

You ideally want to align your core messaging and SEO strategy to create an information architecture or site map with parent and child pages. From an SEO perspective, parent pages are the main pages on the website. Google sees these landing pages as the most important, while child pages are secondary in importance and branch off from the parent pages. So, for example, you might have a landing page providing a general overview of your services that's a parent page and then individual service landing pages for design, copywriting, etc., that are child pages.

As part of creating your website map, you want to avoid orphan landing pages or landing pages that aren't connected to any other landing pages and, therefore, are without a relationship. These landing pages create a poor user experience and aren't great for SEO.

To avoid orphan pages and ensure the right site structure, it's important to think about the customer journey. How will your audience experience your site? What information do they need to see first, and then where would they go? What does the journey look like between when they land on your site and when they submit an inquiry or buy a product?

You want your website to be easy to use and navigate so people can easily and quickly find the information they need. Think of this mapping process as laying the routes. You're designing the routes people will use when experiencing your site to ensure they have the best experience.

Confusing or overly complicated customer journeys will not only frustrate your audience but will also cause them to go elsewhere. I often see websites, especially from large corporations or companies with long histories, which have completely forgotten the user journey and sometimes have hundreds of landing pages. This often happens because different departments have access and control over the website and add content without a clear plan or understanding of what other departments are doing. As a result, the website will become messy, with lots of orphan landing pages or even duplicate landing pages.

Thinking about your user journey is the first step toward identifying the landing pages you need and ensuring your audience has the best experience on your site.

Service, Industry, and Partner Landing Pages

Most websites have standard parent pages like home, about, careers, work with us, etc. These parent pages provide a broad overview of the company but often don't provide in-depth information about capabilities.

As a result, you might want to consider creating dedicated landing pages for each of your services, target industries, or tech partners. Dedicated landing pages allow you to capture specific keywords while also showcasing your expertise within specific industries or with specific tech stacks. Since these pages allow you to target highly relevant keywords, SEO experts generally recommend creating dedicated landing pages.

Step 4: Case Studies

Case studies are an essential part of any website as they're one of the highest-converting pieces of content. By the time someone comes to read your case studies, they're not deciding whether they need your service but whether you're the company for them and whether you can actually solve their problem.

While case studies are essential for every brand, they often get neglected. When teams are busy with day-to-day demands, it's easy to forget about creating new case studies and ensuring that this section of the website always reflects your best work. However, case studies should constantly be reviewed and updated.

I often start a new consulting project by mapping case studies to identify gaps. You ideally want case studies for every service, industry, and tech stack—similar to having dedicated landing pages. So, it can be helpful to look at where you already have case studies and then identify any services, industries, or tech stacks that are missing them.

When creating case studies, it's also important to think about what clients you create case studies with. Case studies provide an opportunity to essentially tell your audience that you've worked with similar brands and attract like-for-like clients. It can be helpful to refer back to your ideal buyer persona and then choose clients that match that persona to create case studies around and showcase your expertise supporting this type of client.

Case Study Troubleshooting

Sometimes, I come across brands that struggle to create case studies, which can happen for several reasons. There's almost always a solution so you can create case studies, and, given that case studies are one of the highest converting pieces of content, it's worth overcoming any challenges or blockers to ensure your website has plenty of high-value case studies to demonstrate your expertise and increase your close rate.

1. Clients Don't Want to Be Featured
Some industries, like cybersecurity, struggle to get clients to agree to create case studies as no one wants to admit they've had a cybersecurity issue or sometimes clients don't want to showcase their providers for fear that competitors might steal their competitive edge. In these cases, creating anonymous case studies can be useful as it still allows you to tell the story of how you helped X company overcome a certain problem and the high-level results you achieved. This story, while perhaps not containing the brand name, still allows you to showcase your expertise and demonstrate your experience solving a particular challenge.

2. The Time Isn't Right
Sometimes, brands struggle to create case studies as they have longer agreements, so projects can stretch for years and never feel fully closed. However, in this case, you can create case studies around specific elements of the project or sprints. Rather than tackling the project as a

whole, focus on subsects of the project or what was achieved in the first six months or a year. Using this approach allows you to showcase your expertise without overwhelming your audience with information by trying to cover the whole project or never being able to because the project hasn't concluded.

3. Client's Won't Sign Off

Another common blocker to case studies is the lack of client agreement. It can be extremely helpful to preempt this problem by making it part of the conversation from the very start of the relationship. For example, by including a clause in the contract to allow for case studies or mentioning wanting to create noteworthy work and a case study during the initial kickoff or implementation call. Raising this early allows you to plant the seed, so it doesn't come as a surprise when you ask later on to create a case study.

Step 5: Blog Content

Blog content plays an important role when initially launching your website but also allows you to grow your domain authority and capture new keywords as you publish more content over time.

When initially creating your website, you want to think about the content you'll use to launch. You don't want a website with an empty insights section. Instead, it's often best to create a bank of content prior to launch that can be used immediately and then create a content strategy for a more regular cadence.

If you're revamping an existing website, this is a good opportunity to review your previous blog content. Rather than doing a straight lift and shift, go through your past content and consider whether it should be part of the new site. Is all the content still relevant? Does any of it need to be updated or removed entirely? What does Google Analytics tell you about previous performance? Is there anything you can do, like ensuring content is properly optimized, to ensure it performs to its best potential?

Once your website is live, it's important to continue creating blog content to showcase your expertise, target new keywords, and continue to provide meaningful content to your audience. Your blog is the best way to increase organic reach over time and build upon the foundation of your website.

Step 6: Setting Up Google Analytics

When creating your website, you want to make sure that you have Google Analytics properly set up. Google Analytics will allow you to capture insights into how your website is performing, how customers are experiencing your site and engaging with content, and how you're acquiring traffic. These insights will shape your marketing strategy and ensure your marketing campaigns are achieving the best results.

I occasionally come across companies that either don't have Google Analytics set up correctly or don't have the right access. Getting this right from the beginning ensures you can track results from day one and take a much more data-led approach to your marketing.

How to Choose a Partner: DIY vs. Agency

Creating a website from scratch or revamping an existing website is a massive undertaking and covers a wide range of disciplines (branding, design, copywriting, and, of course, coding). As a result, you'll most likely need a partner with external providers for at least one element of creating your new website as you either won't have the capabilities in-house or the in-house team will already be busy with other activities.

Agencies or external partners can be helpful for some elements of creating your website, but it's important to pick the right agency and do your due diligence so you don't pick the wrong partner.

Since we originally launched, we've had three different versions of our website. I created our first website myself using WordPress templates. I remember spending hours and hours creating a website, as design isn't something that comes naturally to me. Not only did I spend hours painfully designing a site, but the result wasn't ideal. Looking back, I should have either used a different platform that didn't require coding and was far more user-friendly (like Wix) or invested in the website by partnering with a freelancer. But, at the time, spending any money was far too personal and wasn't an expense I felt we could afford.

For our next website, I worked with a freelance designer to create a website on Wix. While this website was certainly better, it was still limited in design and wasn't truly customized for us. However, I had taken the time to create our core messaging so the copy reflected our offerings and spoke to our customer audience far better than the original site.

Our third website iteration was a far larger investment. We secured a grant from the Scottish government to cover some of the expense but it was still a significant investment. I wanted a website that would position us for future growth and give us a foundation from which to scale. Until this point, we didn't have a brand identity and had a very limited color palette, which made it difficult for our design team to create assets. So, we worked with a brand agency to revamp our visual identity, including new logos, colors, the works. We then partnered with a different agency to do the website, and this is where we went wrong. While the site looked visually appealing, we later discovered a number of technical issues, including website inquiries not coming through to emails. It was shocking and disappointing to have such a poor experience with another agency, but it also taught me the importance of conducting proper research (we had chosen the agency because I was friends with them) and pulling in additional resources to cross-check work for example, using our designer to review to spot any issues.

While working with an agency can make the process of creating a new website easier by taking some of the heavy lifting off your plate, not all agencies are created equal. It's worth speaking to a few different agencies, viewing case studies and getting a third set of eyes on the work (especially in areas where you're perhaps not as confident—like design for me). You also definitely don't want to go with the cheapest option, as your website is one of the most important marketing investments.

Chapter 6

Building Personal Brands and Executive Profiles

I started building a personal brand long before I started building CopyHouse and even before I knew personal branding was a thing. At the time, I was working at a digital marketing agency, getting paid a very low salary of only £12,000 a year. After working there for six months and showing my skills, I asked for a small increase to £14,000 a year, and they turned me down.

However, a few months prior I had had a recruitment agency reach out to me via LinkedIn to ask me to create some blog content and act as a freelance copywriter. I hadn't considered the freelance route as I wanted a more stable career but I wasn't going to turn down the opportunity to create some additional income, so I agreed. Seeing the commercial opportunity early on showed me a way to gain clients, and I slowly began building my client base by creating content on LinkedIn. So, when my request for a small salary increase was rejected, I knew that by leaning on LinkedIn, I could build a freelance portfolio and become independent.

This was the start of my personal branding journey, and today, I have over 13,000 followers, am frequently asked to give keynote speeches, and have built a thriving content marketing agency. I always say that every good thing has come, in some shape or form, via my personal brand.

GETTING STARTED: INVESTING IN LINKEDIN TRAINING

Early on in my LinkedIn journey and before I really understood the platform, I came across the opportunity to join a beta course on creating LinkedIn content. The course provided me with an opportunity to learn the platform, how it worked, and how to create content. Through the course, I gained some of the foundational knowledge for building a personal brand, and investing in training is definitely something I recommend for anyone getting started. It gives you the tools and knowledge needed to overcome the initial fear, demystifies the platform, and helps you feel empowered to start creating content.

I often run LinkedIn training courses for teams, as this can be a good alternative to investing heavily in personal branding for employees. Rather than having content created for their accounts, teaching them how to leverage the platform can be extremely beneficial. After all, teach a man to fish, and they'll never go hungry.

TRANSITIONING FROM SALES-DRIVEN CONTENT

Typically, best practices for social media say that content should be an 80/20 split between direct sales and brand awareness (or top-of-the-funnel) content. However, I didn't know this rule when I first started posting on LinkedIn.

In the beginning, my content was very commercially focused and spoke only about the services I could offer as a freelancer. All content was centered around copywriting and bottom-of-the-funnel content to attract new clients and build my little black book. This was the safe option as I didn't need to put myself out there and share who I really was. I've never been particularly confident on social media and, still, am not active on any other platforms.

However, I had to learn how to embrace this vulnerability and really put myself out there. In order to do so, I needed to become more confident and feel comfortable in my own skin. I started to achieve this about a year and a half into building my personal brand by working with a personal brand coach, who helped me better understand myself and the value I had to offer to my audience.

STRIKING A BALANCE BETWEEN THE COMPANY ACCOUNT AND PERSONAL ACCOUNT

I see many company executives who simply reshare the content their company account posts rather than contributing their own thoughts and opinions. I used to make this mistake as well.

At the beginning of my personal branding journey, all the content I created was directly related to my company. After all, I was a freelancer, so there wasn't a clear divide on social media or in my personal identity between myself and the company. However, as the company grew and I started to feel more confident in myself as an individual, I discovered that I had a voice of my own.

A good personal brand should run parallel to your company account. Your personal brand acts as a top-of-funnel and serves to attract an audience. Content from your personal account is the first thing people see in their social feed, and unsurprisingly, personal accounts perform better on LinkedIn than company accounts. So, you want your personal brand to reflect who you are and share some of the things you're passionate about. For example, talking about leadership, diversity and inclusion or even sharing your story.

Naturally, there'll be some crossover between your personal and company accounts, but this crossover should be minimal. I'd typically recommend that only one or two posts a week are directly related to your company. This content is more top-of-funnel and serves to create a personal connection between you and your audience so they get to know the face behind the brand. After all, people buy from people—not faceless organizations.

However, on the other hand, your company account acts as more mid- and bottom-funnel content. Typically, people will have seen your content from your personal account, clicked on your page, and then moved on to the company page to learn more. As such, your company page is where you'd share information about the company like product updates/releases, new hires, upcoming events, or other important information.

Sometimes, companies will try to reduce the amount of content they need to produce by cutting down on social posts for the company account. However, creating content for your company page is equally important as once they check out your company content, they'll typically click through to the website to learn even more and submit an inquiry to speak to someone on your team.

Identifying Executives Mirroring Technique

If you're a marketing manager helping to create someone else's personal brand, you may need to help identify who in the company you should build a personal brand around. One good technique is to mirror your target audience by using people with similar roles within your company to create a personal brand or executive profile. So, if your target audience is CTOs, build the personal brand around your CTO.

This works because specific roles speak unique languages. CTOs naturally understand and speak the language of other CTOs. They'll enjoy geeking out on the same things and be able to build trust and credibility far more easily than a salesperson. They'll also naturally have a strong network of other CTOs that they've built through their careers, which you can tap into by creating content for them and elevating their profile.

I always recommend building executive profiles around C-suite individuals as they're more bought into the company. When you start building employees' profiles, you'll start attracting an audience—some of which might be other employers who'll try to poach your employees. I've personally experienced this situation with CopyHouse employees, who have started to build their personal brands and then been approached by employers that can offer far higher than market-rate wages. So, I recommend choosing carefully, especially if the company is devoting its own money toward building the individual's personal brand. It can also be helpful to have a contract in place, similar to a training agreement, which ensures you can protect your investment.

PEOPLE BUY FROM PEOPLE

When I started building my personal brand, I focused largely on creating content around copywriting. My early career experiences taught me that being a mom as well as a female were disadvantages and shouldn't be talked about. The problem with creating product-focused content is that it's not personal. Anyone can create content around a specific service or product, as there are lots of people who offer that product/service. But there's only one you, and tapping into that makes you truly unique. It took me a long time to get over my initial hesitations about sharing myself on social media.

We had recently parted ways with a marketing manager so rather than spending money on marketing, I decided to invest by building my personal brand strategy. I worked with a personal brand consultancy to do a deep dive into myself, my personality, and what made me unique. We explored some of the challenges and discrimination I had faced early on in my career and it helped me to reframe these experiences. In many ways, it was like a therapy session and it allowed me to feel more confident sharing my story by being more vulnerable.

After working with the personal brand consultants, I started to share my journey on social media and this is really when my personal brand started to take off. I discovered that many marketing managers and CMOs had similar experiences as women in the workplace or individuals juggling childcare, and having a young daughter wasn't something I needed to be ashamed of. In fact, sharing my story and experiences helped pave the way for other people coming up behind me. I really believe that we have to help others by showing them what is possible and leading the way. I recently brought my daughter to the launch of my podcast to set an example for her as well as to show others that you can be a mom and a CEO.

Throughout this process, I've discovered that people are interested in my expertise and journey of building a business. Sharing my story massively helped me build relationships and connect with my audience.

How Personal Is Too Personal?

I often hear people complain that LinkedIn has become too much like Facebook. By this, they mean that people share too much personal information, often personal information that the person criticizing would feel uncomfortable sharing themselves.

While there's certainly a fine balance to strike, I tend to think about LinkedIn as the workplace. After all, it is a professional social media network. As such, I share things on LinkedIn that I would be comfortable sharing with my coworkers. Not all things are work appropriate, like perhaps the massive party and resulting hangover you had at the weekend. Instead, I think about the stories I'm already telling when I meet someone networking or speak with one of my team members.

If you feel comfortable telling these stories offline in professional settings, they're usually also appropriate for social media.

However, saying that, I'm also aware of the image social media can present. It can be tempting only to showcase the "good stuff" and show a glossy image of your work life or running a business. But this is almost never the case, as all businesses have struggles and challenges. Pushing beyond the glossy image and sharing the struggles is also equally important for creating a realistic image. I'm still working on this myself, as I still find it scary to share some of the pitfalls of running an agency publicly.

BENEFITS OF PERSONAL BRANDING

I've seen firsthand the benefits of personal branding, and most of the good things that have happened at CopyHouse have come via my personal brand in some shape or form—be it new experiences, employees, or clients.

Building your personal brand, or helping an executive build their personal brand, gives you a platform for sharing your thoughts and opinions and allows you to stay top of mind with your audience. Very few people will wake up and go onto your website to read your latest blog, but they will wake up, reach for their mobile, and go onto social media. I know it's one of the first things I look at every morning upon waking and every evening before bed (bad habits die hard). So, creating content from your personal brand can help you get in front of this audience and unlock some serious opportunities.

I believe in the power of personal branding so much that I launched it as a new service at CopyHouse and started to help entrepreneurs and C-suite executives build their personal brands. Most of these individuals are quite introverted, as is often the case in the tech industry, so they wouldn't feel comfortable creating their own content. However, by creating content for them, I've unlocked some of the same opportunities.

Building your personal brand is often low-hanging fruit as you start to see results relatively quickly, or at least much quicker than building expertise via long-form content. As such, social media is often a good place for companies to start building brand awareness as it allows them to establish their expertise and become known for a specific product or service, network and build relationships with other thought leaders, attract employees and potential new clients to your company, and unlock new opportunities for speaking engagements.

I've seen so many opportunities come via my personal brand that it's branched off into a new company, Kathryn Strachan Ltd., to handle all the speaking engagements, consulting gigs, NED roles, and things that don't fit neatly within CopyHouse. Kathryn Strachan Ltd., which now runs alongside CopyHouse, is a business in its own right, unlocking opportunities for CopyHouse as consulting clients inevitably need content.

Control Your Reputation

One of the key benefits of having a personal brand is the ability to control and shape your reputation. Traditionally, reputation relied almost entirely on what others had to say about you. Rather than relying on the good words of others, you can take a more active approach by sharing your achievements, thought leadership, and values. In other words, personal branding allows you to back up your reputation and, therefore, control its direction.

While we all hope that nothing bad ever happens, if a PR crisis does strike your business, you then have a different side to the story. People will have already gotten to know you and have a relationship with you so they then don't only see the negative image portrayed in the media. Creating a personal brand allows you to mitigate this risk by building relationships *before* the sh★t hits the fan.

Attract Top Talent

Personal branding not only attracts prospective clients but also helps to attract new employees. Employees want to know who they'll work for and whether a potential employer has a good work environment and is an empathetic leader. Research shows that younger generations are increasingly opting for companies with shared values and good leadership. Sometimes, these traits can outstrip being able to offer the highest salary.

We always had a hard time competing for talent as we're not VC-backed, so we can't offer above-market rates. While I always want to pay everyone fairly, sometimes, especially during the Great Resignation, I couldn't compete with the salaries being offered by large tech companies. I remember having Revolut poach three of our employees and attempt to poach a fourth.

However, my personal brand has a large influence on my ability to attract new employees and retain existing ones. Obviously, my personal brand is backed up and reflective of my actual approach to leadership, but having a platform to share my thoughts, ideas, and values certainly helps. With most B2B industries experiencing talent shortages, personal branding for company executives should be taken more seriously.

CONSISTENCY IS KEY

While personal branding can definitely be a low-hanging fruit, especially when you first start to tap into an existing network, achieving the juicy results takes time and consistent effort. You really need to post four to five times a week for the algorithm to work best and produce the right results.

Achieving consistency can be very difficult, and there were weeks when I didn't feel like posting. Maybe I was feeling a bit rundown or stressed out, but coming up with unique content every day can feel like a burden. However, I found that the best approach was to create content ahead of time, so every Sunday, I sat down and created my posts for the week. I then scheduled them so I didn't need to think about it in the mornings as I was almost always busy and in the flow of work by 9 am every day. I also kept a Google doc for social post ideas that I added to during the week.

It has taken consistency and patience to grow my network and achieve results. Building a personal brand requires consistent commitment and dedication, but the opportunities it unlocks are worth the effort.

EXPANDING PERSONAL BRANDING BEYOND LINKEDIN

LinkedIn is a natural place to start building your personal brand, but a good personal brand needs to extend far beyond LinkedIn. Personal branding should include your network (see next chapter), relation-ships and a whole host of additional marketing activities. As you get going, you'll start to attract opportunities for speaking engagements, podcast appearances, and even media coverage. You'll also probably start to think about other ways to elevate your brand, like hosting your own podcast, writing a book, or having a personal website.

My approach to personal branding has certainly changed over time as my brand has grown and as we've started to understand our audi-ence even better. I'm a big fan of fishing where the fish are, and I've used this strategy to align my personal brand to connect with the right audiences on the platforms where they already are. After all, it's a lot easier to go to them than to get them to come to you.

Today, my approach includes being active on LinkedIn and Instagram, holding non-executive and advisory roles to build a port-folio career, hosting my podcast, Tech Marketers Uncorked, contribut-ing thought leadership to external publications, speaking at events and on podcasts, being active in communities aimed at our target audi-ence, hosting our own events and being a serial networker. While this approach is obviously quite extensive, it's been built over time and has taken over four years to get to this point.

Building a Speaking Career

When you start creating content on LinkedIn and building a personal brand, you'll naturally start to attract requests for speaking engage-ments or appearances on podcasts. Event organizers and podcast hosts want to feature people who already have a following, as this helps them promote their event or show. As a result, getting speaking engagements without a personal brand is extremely difficult, and you'll likely need the personal brand before you can start attracting these opportunities.

Speaking on stage or a podcast takes practice to get right, but the more you practice, the better you become. I secured my first speaking event at an SEO meetup before the pandemic and before I started properly building CopyHouse. I used to have a recording of my talk, and it wasn't very good. I was visibly nervous, didn't know my lines, and kept having to refer back to the slides. Looking back, I can see how far I've come.

I've been quite lucky. I started building my speaking career before the pandemic, which meant that many of my speaking events during the pandemic were online. It's easier to practice speaking online, as you can't see the audience and have a direct view of your slides. As a result, speaking at webinars is often an easier introduction to speaking than speaking on stage or at a big event.

Once you know your topics and the stories that land with the audience, it's then easier to take it live. By this point, you should also have good momentum and be asked to speak at bigger and bigger events. The next step is to bring your expertise to life in front of a live audience that you can actually see.

Ideally, your first live event will be a panel rather than a keynote. Panels are easier as you'll be on stage with multiple people and only need to answer the question confidently. You don't need to craft an entire narrative, and all eyes won't be on you. Once you master the panel, it's easier to transition to the keynote and gradually build your speaking portfolio this way.

One pro tip for building a speaking career is to make sure to capture the content via recording and pictures. You want to be able to share your engagements on social and also capture your experience speaking to pitch in to larger events and create a speaker reel to promote your speaking services.

Networking

Another key element to building a personal brand is building a community via networking and getting to know your audience. I've personally set a goal of meeting 50 new people every month and have used LinkedIn to stay in touch with these individuals.

I make sure to add everyone I meet in real life to LinkedIn, which then allows me to create a black book of everyone I know while also staying top of mind by creating content and appearing in their feeds. I also, likewise, use LinkedIn to reach out to new contacts (not in a sales way) to build relationships and see whether they fancy meeting up for a virtual coffee.

While creating content on LinkedIn can be massively helpful for building relationships at scale and keeping in touch with people, nothing beats actually spending time with someone and getting to know them.

DON'T LET PERFECTION STAND IN THE WAY OF PROGRESS

I think one of the biggest barriers for people to create their personal brands is being worried about pushing something live that isn't perfect. After all, social media can seem like such a cruel place. Social media has a relatively short shelf life, so as long as you're not racist, homophobic, or anything else mean and offensive, you'll be fine.

It takes time to discover the type of content that works with your audience. So, your first post is highly unlikely to go viral, but over time, you'll start to gain traction and build a strong following. As you get going, it becomes easier to create content that hits the mark and gets good results.

I often recommend that you think of these early days as prepping the algorithm, testing what works and what doesn't, getting to know your audience, and refining your approach. Most importantly, don't be so hard on yourself, as your first posts don't need to be perfect.

Chapter 7

Your Network Is Your Net Worth

I remember my first networking event in a conference room at a big hotel in Edinburgh. I was one of the only women in the room (out of about 50 people) and didn't know anyone. It was awkward and cringe-worthy, and I almost never went back to a networking event. When something is awkward and uncomfortable, it's easy to avoid doing it.

However, about a year into building CopyHouse, my mentor challenged me to meet a target of 50 new connections every single month. At first, this felt like a staggering target, but over time, it got easier, and now I consistently hit and exceed this target. Over the years, I've met thousands of people and have experienced the benefits of networking firsthand.

Networking and spending time building relationships have had one of the biggest tangible impacts on CopyHouse. I've been surprised by the number of people who were happy to have a coffee and share their wisdom, make recommendations, or open doors for me. Businesses are not islands and I really believe that we need a strong network around us to really grow.

As the old saying goes, "It's not what you know, but who."

50 NEW PEOPLE EVERY MONTH

One of my early advisors set a target of meeting 50 new people every month. At first, I thought he was crazy, as that seemed like such a huge number. But it was the middle of the pandemic, and I was hungry to make CopyHouse work. Since work was still fully remote and in-person events had ground to a halt, I had to make this target through one-to-one online calls. I have one friend who ensured his company survived the pandemic by meeting over 200 new people every month, and his business continues to fly today with a strong community and over 50 in-person events a year.

Networking has certainly changed since the beginning of the pandemic. I no longer need to have one-to-one calls with everyone but can go to an event and easily meet 10 people in one night. If I then go to four events a month, it suddenly becomes a lot easier to reach that target.

The more you network, the more achievable and enjoyable it becomes. You begin to recognize friendly faces at events, get invited to other events, or are introduced to other relevant people. Like building a snowball and pushing it downhill, organic momentum gets easier as you consistently put in the effort.

OVERCOMING INITIAL FEARS AND HESITATIONS

If you're new to networking, it's natural to feel a little nervous at your first event. I felt the same way when I started attending events, but as I attended more events, I naturally started to meet more people. Now, there's at least one friendly face at every event.

However, I still sometimes don't want to go to an event. Maybe I'm feeling tired or under the weather, or my social battery is drained. When I feel this way, I like to play a little game with myself and set a challenge that I need to meet before I go home. For example, telling myself I can go home after I speak to 10 new people or make a circle around the room and meet one person at every point. I also sometimes bring a small stack of business cards (I know they are so old-fashioned-) and go home once I've handed out all my cards. Setting challenges helps make the experience a little more fun when

I'm not feeling social and helps overcome some of the initial fears and hesitations.

GETTING STARTED WITH NETWORKING

I was asked recently by a graduate how they could make a good impression within their new role and get up to speed quickly. My answer? Ask people for coffee.

You'll be surprised by how willing people are to help. We've all been at the beginning of our careers or in a new role and needed a helping hand. People far more senior than us have taken the time to catch up over coffee and spend time sharing their wisdom. I personally think that most people enjoy being asked for their expertise and are flattered by the offer and what's the worst that can happen?

If you ask someone for a coffee, the worst that can happen is that they'll ignore you or not respond. So, there's little risk with potentially huge rewards.

I got my start in copywriting by asking local agency owners and copywriters for a coffee and catching up. These conversations provided me with knowledge and insights that helped shape my career and even opened up some initial positions. After all, most junior positions and internships are filled by people the hiring managers/companies already know, as they get hundreds of applications when recruiting for these positions.

Cutting Through the Noise and Perfecting Your Elevator Pitch

When you're networking, you need to be able to quickly tell people what you do, who you are, what they should remember you for, and what you are looking to gain from networking.

Over the years, I've met thousands of people and business owners, so I have heard many business propositions. At a networking event, you need to process a lot of information quickly and be able to remember people later. You also want to know quickly how you can help someone, who you can introduce them to, and what opportunities would be relevant.

Sometimes, I'd meet business owners who'd say they run a full-service digital marketing agency that's industry-agnostic. I think this is perhaps one of the least helpful responses as it tells me very little about them or how I can help.

So, before you go to a networking event, make sure you know your elevator pitch. It should be a one- or two-sentence summary of who you are. Practice your elevator pitch a few times with friends and family before your next event. Remember, you want your messaging to be clear, specific, and memorable.

Play to Your Strengths

I've always had a rather bubbly and extroverted personality; I think because I originally grew up in the US. Americans are known for their big personalities and ability to make friends rather quickly (unlike the British, who are more reserved). My husband always made fun of me for making friends with the person sitting next to me on an airplane. He would say that you can't make a new friend in a few hours, but I certainly can.

I've used my personality to my advantage, especially when selling in the British market. British people are always a little taken aback and flattered that I want to be their friend (and I genuinely do). I met one of my good friends on a sales call when I invited them to an event I was going to that evening, and the rest is history.

However, networking can be far more challenging if you're not naturally extroverted. For more introverted people, you can still network and build connections, but rather than going to a big event, and perhaps your networking takes the shape of one-to-one online calls. Once you get comfortable speaking to people online, you might start attending events where you already know people and feel comfortable.

Just remember that most people are nice, and people, especially at networking events, are there to meet new people. So, it's not awkward or rude to go up to someone new and introduce yourself. They're probably expecting it to some degree—they are at a networking event, after all.

Giving a Helping Hand

Every time I meet someone new, I try to help them in some way. Perhaps it's introducing them to someone relevant, sharing recommendations, or helping them address a particular challenge. Lending a helping hand helps make a good impression and creates reciprocity. So, for example, if you introduce someone, they're far more likely to introduce you to someone they know in turn.

At the beginning of my networking journey, I used this method of creating reciprocity. I'd introduce every person I met to at least three people in my network. They then introduced me to others, helping me build the initial momentum to reach my goal of meeting 50 new people every month.

Stay Connected

Once you meet someone at a networking event, you want to stay connected and continue to build the relationship after the event. If you're building your network at scale, it'll be easy to forget people and what they do. I started building a database of everyone I met using keywords for what they did and what sort of opportunities they were looking for. This allowed me to search the database to find the right people and then create connections much more easily.

I could also use this database to invite them to upcoming events, let them know if I was going to be in their city or add them to our newsletter to send regular updates. I also added them on LinkedIn so they could see my content and become part of my online network.

While I no longer have a physical database, I do use my LinkedIn connections as my digital Rolodex. Every time I meet someone new,

I make sure I connect with them on LinkedIn and then use the search function to search through my contacts to find people in a specific location, industry, or role. This is extremely useful for staying connected and being able to connect with the right people at the right time.

Naturally, not everyone you meet networking will provide value to you or your business. You have to kiss a lot of frogs. But by meeting so many people every month, you're likely to meet plenty of people who will make a big difference and are certainly worth keeping in touch with.

BUILDING YOUR ONLINE NETWORK

Building relationships happens offline, over lunch, or at in-person events, as well as online, and in today's world, it's impossible to ignore the importance of online connections. I've personally used LinkedIn to reach out to people I wanted to get to know, invite them to in-person events, and build connections. I've never met some of my LinkedIn connections in real life, but they comment on my content and help champion my work.

Growing Your Network

There are a few ways to grow your online network. You can send connection requests to people who match your target audience, like CMOs or marketing managers. Having these people in your network can be beneficial, as they'll learn about you and your work through your content. If they're already familiar with you, it's much easier to ask for a coffee or have them say yes to an upcoming event.

You can also be stricter with your LinkedIn account and only send connection requests to people you know. Some people believe this is the best way to engage your network and achieve the best results on your content. It also makes it easier to remember people. I don't personally subscribe to this method and sometimes see the downside as people will see I'm connected with someone and mistakenly believe that I know them.

The third method, which I *do* subscribe to, is to send connection requests to people you know and people who engage with your content or visit your profile. I keep a close eye on my LinkedIn page views and then send people connection requests. I also make sure that I connect with everyone I meet—whether we meet over a virtual coffee or in person. This allows me to build a network of people I know and people who are interested in knowing more about me.

Regardless of the method you choose, you'll need to send connection requests in some form to build an online network and start building a following on your social media network.

Nurturing Your Network

Like all relationships, building an online following can't be a one-way street; it requires nurturing. For example, suppose someone takes the time to comment on your post. In that case, it's important to reply as this not only keeps the conversation going but also encourages them to comment on future posts and increases your results. You want to engage with and get to know your audience.

You should also spend time commenting on other people's posts. Share your thoughts on the content in your feed, help celebrate others' achievements, or offer solutions to their problems. Commenting is a key way to build and nurture your online network.

Another good way to build relationships is by sending non-sales updates via LinkedIn Messenger. While most people cringe at outbound LinkedIn messages, and this is certainly true for hard sales, sending a soft-touch automated message that tells people what you've been up to and asks them to tell you about them can be a good approach. I've run campaigns like this, and it's started some important conversations with people, some of whom became clients.

MY APPROACH TO NETWORKING

My approach to networking has changed over time, and as I've developed a better understanding of my audience. I've learned about some of the best ways to build relationships as well as the networks and communities worth being part of.

Build Relationships over Lunches and Dinners

I've found lunches and dinners to be one of the most effective ways to build relationships. Lunch allows you to spend time getting to know people and learning more than you would on an online call, which is a far more formal and transactional environment. Lunches, while more of a soft approach to sales, has allowed me to build stronger relationships and unlock business opportunities. So much so that I spend a lot of my time eating lunch in nice restaurants and have become the self-proclaimed "queen of lunches."

I now host private, invite-only roundtable events, which allow me to bring people together and create connections. These events allow me to build relationships with potential clients without going for the direct sale, bring people together, and create a memorable experience to create brand advocates. Hosting CMO roundtables has been one of the ways we've built a community around CopyHouse.

Choose Your Network

When I started networking, I wasn't very selective about the networks or communities I joined. I mostly followed my fellow agency friends by joining industry bodies like BIMA or the Alliance of Independent Agencies. However, I realized that we were part of several similar networks and weren't seeing a great deal of value as we almost never work directly with agencies.

It's easy to get involved in many networks and communities, but it's worth thinking about the ones you're part of. All communities take time to nurture and grow, and you'll get out what you put in. Given my limited time, I needed to be more strategic with my network and communities. So, we looked at our audience and where they were spending their time.

Since we're sector-specific and normally work directly with brands, we then focused on building connections in communities with CMOs and brands. Joining communities like Chief, the Payment Association, etc. allowed us to get in front of our audience or, in other words, to fish where the fish are.

Staying Top of Mind

I rely quite heavily on my LinkedIn content to stay in touch with the people I meet through networking. By adding them to my network and then posting regularly (four to five times a week), I appear in their feed. Since most people are on LinkedIn daily, they see my content relatively regularly, and I can stay top of mind. It also gives me a way to update them on developments within the company or my own career. Naturally, I'm one of the first people they think of when a relevant opportunity arises.

Having a strong personal brand backed by networking and real-life connections is a powerful solution. Building relationships online and offline supercharges my marketing efforts and creates a consistent stream of leads.

stages of their career and addressing challenges like negotiating a new salary, planning their career, and making big life decisions. Being able to share my experiences and wisdom with her has helped her view these experiences from a different perspective and has also reinforced some of my knowledge as well as my belief in myself. Teaching is one of the best ways to take you back to the basics and remind you how much you know and how far you've come.

Being a marketing manager, CMO, or any role can be lonely, and representation can be poor. Very few companies give senior marketers a seat at the table, and these people are often so busy building brands and promoting other people that they don't get the same limelight. However, acting as a mentor or finding a mentor is a great way to overcome this challenge and have role models who have been in your position before.

There are some great schemes out there to facilitate this, but you can also reach out to people you admire and ask if they'd be your mentor or at least grab a cup of coffee. Very few people will say no to coffee or lunch. Plus, what's the worst that can happen?

FINDING A COMMUNITY FOR GROWTH AND DEVELOPMENT

Everyone needs a support network and being part of a community can be a great way to connect with and learn from peers. Ideally, try to join a community where people have a shared problem or interest, similar roles, or approaches/lifestyles. For example, CMOs might try the CMO Alliance. Communities often also offer additional benefits like training courses, which can be great for learning and development.

Being part of a community can be a great way to put your lived experiences into context. It can be easy, especially if you're part of a small team, to think that your challenges are unique or that other companies don't have the same problems. However, marketing managers and CMOs often experience the same challenges across the board by trying to get stakeholders' sign-off, working with reduced budgets, or trying to support a whole company with limited resources. Since I'm lucky enough to speak to many CMOs and marketing managers on a daily basis, I see these same problems over and over again. When you're in the thick of things, it can be difficult to have the same perspective, but speaking to others in similar roles at different companies not only gives you perspective but can be a good way to find creative solutions. At the very least, you'll have someone to vent to who understands your problems.

Being part of a community is also a great way to learn from peers who may have different expertise but shared interests. Learning from others in the industry helps build relationships and expand your horizons on different ways to build marketing campaigns, best practices, and emerging trends. Since there is no one way to approach marketing, getting a second opinion or different viewpoint is excellent for expanding your knowledge and skill set.

WORKING WITH AN ADVISOR OR CONSULTANT

Depending on where you are in your journey of building a brand, an advisor or consultant can be extremely helpful. Before you can work with an agency, freelancer, or even hire a marketing manager, you need to have an understanding of the big vision for your company's marketing. Where do you see high growth potential? Who is your target audience, and how are you going to reach them? What does the big picture look like?

A marketing advisor or consultant can help you lay some of this initial groundwork. Think of them as the surveyors. It's their job to know the lay of the land and advise you on the best course for getting to your final destination. They've traveled this path before, so know what you should bring on your journey and how to ensure you can reach your destination safely.

I started working as a marketing consultant as we'd often get companies coming to us that knew they wanted to raise brand awareness but weren't sure how to go about it. As a content marketing agency, it was difficult for CopyHouse to help. While inevitably, you'll need content in some form, you need the big picture before you know what type of content you need, whether you should work with an agency or in-house, etc. I, however, could help these brands define their larger marketing strategy, carve out a budget, and build a marketing team, which sometimes includes hiring a marketing manager or partnering with an agency.

AGENCY, FREELANCER, OR INTERNAL TEAM MEMBER?

Once you have an idea of your larger marketing strategy, you need to decide how to implement it and whether you'll need to hire additional team members, work with a freelancer, or partner with an agency. Each option has pros and cons and typically depends on the overall business strategy and the extent of your requirements.

In-House Team Members

Hiring in-house team members can be a good option as it gives you greater control over the final product. However, if you already have a marketing manager, your in-house hires will be far more specific, such as a social media executive or copywriter. If you have high demands around social or content, this can be particularly effective, but most companies, especially in the early stages of building their brand, have a full-time requirement.

You'll also need to add this person to the payroll, which comes with additional costs of employee benefits and government taxes. It's also normally much more difficult to get rid of this person if they don't perform as expected or if the company suffers a downturn, as you'd need to go through a formal redundancy process.

I've previously supplemented CopyHouse's marketing team by hiring a content executive to support our marketing manager with content production. While this worked when times were good, when the company went through a downturn, it was a role we could no longer justify and needed to make redundant. More recently, we've hired a marketing intern, who provides support to our marketing manager with some of the more basic tasks—however, junior marketing people (like all junior employees) require quite a lot more handholding, support and development so while this move has been largely beneficial, it's also distracted our marketing manager.

Freelancers

Working with a freelancer can also be a good option, as it allows you to get specific support without needing to hire a full-time employee. Supplementing your staff with multiple freelancers can allow you to tap into a wider variety of skill sets and create a more well-balanced marketing mix. Sometimes, freelancers are cheaper than agencies.

However, freelance resources can be difficult to manage as they're still a one-person team, so the good ones are often booked up. Largely speaking, they don't have sophisticated processes for managing projects as there's no client service team, which isn't ideal for larger projects. Juggling multiple freelancers can also become cumbersome for your marketing manager as it means lots of moving parts. Pricing can also vary widely depending on the freelancer, and not all offer the same cost savings.

I've used freelancers as part of our marketing resources. We have a brilliant freelance designer whom we have a long-standing relationship with, who supports design projects and a freelance copywriter who helps with content. Working with freelancers has allowed us to have dedicated resources so projects don't get delayed for our clients (as was often the case with our internal team) and stick to a relatively small budget. However, our copywriting and design requirements are relatively minimal, so this approach works.

Agency

I'm obviously biased, but I think agencies are great. They offer access to a wider range of skills by virtue of being studios, have more sophisticated processes, as most have dedicated client service teams, and generally produce higher-quality, larger projects.

However, working with an agency can be more expensive than a freelancer or in-house hire, depending on the freelancer and role. While you get access to a wide range of skills and will have a team working on your account, most agencies are crazy, unstable places, which naturally means there's a higher turnover than other companies. So, you may see a lot of turnover while working with an agency, which means having lots of different people working on your account. Agencies, however, should be able to facilitate this turnover rather smoothly as it's relatively common.

Some agencies may not take smaller, lesser-known brands seriously, as you either pay less or have less impact than their blue-chip clients. So, even though you may feel like you're giving them a hefty chunk of your budget, you might not get the service or support you expect.

We've worked with agencies on a few occasions for brand, PR, and our website. Some of these experiences have been better than others. Our brand agency did a fantastic job creating CopyHouse 2.0 and helping position us for our next stage of growth, but they had come highly recommended and had a strong track record in branding for agencies. Our work with the design agency produced shocking results that were far below standards. So much so that leads from our website weren't coming through to our email for six months, which had a direct impact on our revenue. While this agency belonged to a friend of mine, I admittedly didn't speak to many agencies or really consider my options—something I definitely regretted later on.

While I have plenty of horror stories, agencies generally have a positive impact on marketing. They give you access to a wide range of skills and can help you understand the larger market as they work with and have experience within the sector.

WORKING WITH AN AGENCY

Unless you're going to rely exclusively on in-house or freelance talent, you'll likely need to partner with an agency. Agencies come in all shapes and sizes and cover all disciplines and can be extremely helpful for covering gaps within your existing team or adding outside perspective on best practices across the industry.

However, finding the right agency can be a bit of a minefield. With so many options to choose from, it can be easy to choose the wrong one. Working with the wrong agency will make the work feel like pulling teeth, and either nothing will get accomplished, or the wrong things will get accomplished, producing poor results and causing you to lose time and money.

Prerequisites to Choosing an Agency

Before you choose an agency, you need to set the foundations to make the process as easy as possible. You should start by defining the budget, checking internal processes, and identifying the must-have requirements.

Defining the Budget

Your budget will determine the type of agency you can work with and whether you can work with one at all. Agency fees can vary greatly, and the larger agencies naturally have much higher fees. It's very helpful to know the budget before starting to look for agencies and using this to shape your approach. Not having a budget is a bit like throwing a dart in the dark and will make your search more difficult.

Normally, if I know the budget, I can propose suitable solutions and work to reverse engineer the quote to allow us to get the best results while staying within the budget. Without this information, I can only work on best practices and ideal situations or what I'd love to do with the brand. You may not be able to start with the ideal or perfect setup, but budget restraints might mean you start smaller and then work your way up. This is totally fine, but it is helpful to know in advance.

Procurement Processes

Before you begin looking for agencies, it's important to check internal processes and understand the requirements for sourcing a new partner. You may be restricted to a pre-approved list of suppliers or need to produce multiple quotes for any project over a certain financial threshold. I've seen a host of different procurement processes, ranging from extremely complex and taking six months to complete to requiring multiple quotes. Knowing this process beforehand can allow you to streamline it and also make sure you plan for any hurdles you might encounter when onboarding your new agency.

Must-Have Requirements

Before you begin your search, it's also important to understand exactly *what* you're looking for. Hopefully, you already have an overall marketing strategy and a clear understanding of where you need support and the type of service you're looking for. Most agencies have specialties as very few agencies do everything equally well. I never really believe that an agency is truly full-service, especially when they only have a small team. So, it's helpful to start by knowing what you're looking for—otherwise, it can be like finding a needle in a haystack.

Size

You then want to think about any additional requirements. For example, do you need an agency that's a particular size? Bigger does not always mean better, especially if you're a start-up or scale-up. Most big agencies will have big blue-chip clients, so being a small or relatively unknown brand means that you're unlikely to receive the same level of service and attention. Ideally, you should choose an agency that aligns with your current size, so if you're a mid-size company, choose a mid-size agency.

Location

You might want to consider if you need an agency in a certain location, perhaps for in-person projects like video filming or if you prefer face-to-face interactions. Location isn't everything, but it can be important depending on your requirements.

Industry Expertise

You might also want to consider whether you require industry expertise. What industry do you work in? Does the agency have experience in this industry? I meet a lot of future clients who try working with a generalist agency but aren't happy with the results they achieve and the amount of handholding required to get the agency up to speed on their industry. It's not surprising when you're working in a complicated or complex space. After all, it isn't easy to wake up and write about blockchain. However, working with an agency that already has a track record in that sector can be helpful for onboarding and getting quick results.

Agency Pitch

If you haven't sourced an agency before, there are some things you can do to make the process easier and avoid agency blowback.

One of the biggest cardinal sins is requesting pitches from multiple agencies. Putting together pitches requires a lot of time, resources, and money from agencies. They don't typically mind doing it, and it can be a good way to judge the process as you get to see an agency's work in action before you buy. It's the closest you'll get to "try before you buy." However, since a pitch requires the agency's resources, it's also important to be respectful of their time and effort.

I normally recommend keeping the number of pitch requests to three. Although you may have early-stage conversations with multiple agencies, narrow it down to your top three and then ask them to pitch.

When asking them to pitch, be clear about your requirements and judging criteria. There are thousands of ways to skin a cat, and it'll make your job more difficult if the agencies don't have a brief to work from. Giving them a brief means that it'll be a more direct comparison so that you won't be comparing apples to oranges but apples to apples.

After the pitch, make sure to provide feedback. There is nothing worse for an agency than spending days and money on a pitch and then being ghosted. If they've taken the time to put together a pitch (or even a proposal), make sure to tell them how they did, what they could do to improve, and how they could win next time.

You never want to burn bridges with agencies as you don't know when you might need to call on them again or where they might crop up.

HOW TO CHOOSE THE RIGHT AGENCY

With so many agencies out there, how exactly do you go about choosing the right one? Especially if it's your first time choosing an agency, there are some things you might want to think about or do.

Recommendations

I almost always source agencies based on referrals or recommendations. While this approach certainly isn't foolproof, it's often safer to work with an agency that someone recommends or that you've worked with before. I normally rely on my existing connections when finding an agency for a consulting client, as I'm less likely to have a bad experience. However, if you don't know any agencies and no one has any specific recommendations, checking out the agency's case studies is the next best thing.

Case Studies and Samples

One of the first things you'll want to check out is the agency's case studies and any samples of previous work. Not all work, especially strategic work, can be shared directly, but sector samples should give you an idea of how well they understand your space. Case studies help to build this credibility and show you who they've worked with previously, as well as the challenges they've helped clients overcome and the results they've achieved. You definitely need to check out case studies before working with any agency.

Meet the Team

Before working with an agency, make sure you meet the team who'll be working on your project. Often, agencies will only present the salesperson or some of the more senior leaders. But you'll want to know who will be working with you and meet them at least once before signing a contract. It's not always normal practice to bring these individuals into sales calls as they're often busy, so make sure you ask for a chemistry call with the people who'll be working with you.

Chapter 9

Becoming Recognized as an Industry Expert with Content Marketing

When you're building your brand, you'll naturally want to start producing content to showcase your expertise and raise brand awareness. Almost all companies have brilliant people who work there. These are the people who make ideas come to life, delight clients and help to drive your company forward. Most of the time, they're so busy that they don't have time or interest in creating content or contributing to marketing efforts.

While you can start to build their profiles with personal branding (as we discussed previously), social media, as short-form content, only allows you to capture their expertise to a degree. Short-form content restricts you from diving in deeply into a topic. So, you'll want to pair it with more long-form content.

Long-form content like thought leadership articles, whitepapers, or blogs gives you the depth to get into the meat of a subject. With a greater word count, you can explore topics to showcase the expanse of your expertise and highlight unique viewpoints. It's the perfect opportunity to have longer, more meaningful conversations with your audience and, of course, leverage SEO to increase organic reach.

PROBLEMS WITH PR

Many brands initially turn to PR when they want to position themselves as thought leaders and increase their organic reach. However, implementing PR tactics *before* you have developed your brand and started to build brand awareness can feel like an uphill battle.

Journalists, naturally and understandably so, want to cover brands and people who are already known or have a strong following. If a well-known brand like Revolut or Monzo implements a four-day workweek, it'll be all over the media. If an unknown brand launches the same scheme, it's unlikely to appear in any media outlets. Unless you're doing something truly unique or groundbreaking, it can be difficult to attract media attention before you have a strong brand.

I have met many brands that want to build brand awareness and hire a PR agency. At this point, they normally haven't done any content for their own website, built the brands for their company leaders, or sometimes even have a website. PR is seen as the magic bullet for creating brand awareness. However, many times, the PR agency struggles to produce any tangible results as they either don't secure any media placements or the placements are in low-quality content mills. While PR can achieve some great results, it's often a good idea to ensure you build your foundations first.

I had this experience and made the same mistake with CopyHouse. About a year into building our brand, I wanted to accelerate our brand awareness, so I hired a PR agency that specialized in tech. Since they specialized in our sector, I thought they'd be able to secure placements, and we'd be appearing in *Forbes* in no time. This was far from what happened. Initially, we secured a few placements (mostly with low-quality publications), and we then asked them to focus on higher-tier media outlets, at which point the results stopped entirely. We spent months paying the PR agency with no results. With PR, you often won't have a retainer against deliverables but against a set amount of time that the team will spend pitching to journalists. After a few months, we finally got tired of not seeing results and parted ways with them.

We then hired a copywriter to focus on our own content and increase the brand via our blog and social channels. By creating content on a regular basis, we were able to grow our brand and then media requests started to flow our way. Once we had a stronger brand, we were then asked to appear in publications and found that we were able to naturally attract these opportunities by having a strong brand. The lesson here is that sometimes, you need to focus on setting the right foundations and building your brand before securing media placements.

THOUGHT-LEADERSHIP CONTENT

Thought-leadership content, by its nature, is based on subject-matter experts and requires having a unique opinion or approach. It allows you to showcase your credibility within your organization or partner with external subject-matter experts to increase your reach. Creating thought-leadership content is a good way to build your brand, as it allows you to stick your flag in the ground and stand out from competitors. Even if other people offer the same service or product, no one thinks like you and your team. Showing your audience that you not only understand their problems but know exactly how to fix them and have years of experience behind you also builds credibility. As such, thought-leadership content should be part of any brand.

Choosing Your Thought Leaders

Before you can begin creating thought-leadership content, you need to choose your thought leaders. Whose expertise will you draw from? What expert opinions do you want to feature?

Sometimes, there will be natural subject-matter experts within the business, but other times, you may not have the internal expertise. If you lack internal expertise, there are a few ways you can overcome this challenge, such as showcasing the expertise of your partners/clients or sourcing from the wider industry for a broader reach and appeal.

Internal Thought Leaders

When choosing your internal thought leaders, consider subject-matter experts who naturally speak the same language as your audience. For example, if you're targeting CTOs, leveraging their insights makes sense. You also want to choose people who already have a strong network, as it's much easier to build from an existing network than from the ground up. Elevating their profile, even if they haven't been active previously, will then be much easier.

Generally, I recommend avoiding anyone from the sales team unless, of course, you're focused on selling to other salespeople. While salespeople are great, they often speak a language that doesn't directly connect with your audience and can be perceived as off-putting, as everyone is expecting them to sell to them.

External Thought Leaders

Sometimes, companies either don't have people internally who can act as subject-matter experts or want to expand their reach and collaborate with others in the industry. In these cases, it can be a good idea to partner with subject-matter experts from outside the organization.

When a company is broadening into a new sector, building a new technology, or even new territory, it may not have anyone internally who can act as a subject-matter expert. But this doesn't mean you can't create thought-leadership content. One way to get around this challenge is by partnering with external thought leaders. Do you have anyone in your network whom you'd like to showcase? Perhaps a client, partner, prospect, or even industry influencer? This allows you to get around the internal hurdle and begin building your expertise around a new subject.

Leveraging external thought leaders is also a useful approach for strengthening industry relationships and increasing the reach of your content. Most people enjoy being interviewed as it's a bit of an ego stroke and it allows them to speak about a topic they're passionate about to someone genuinely interested. So, you'll be surprised by the people who'll willingly contribute. Plus, what's the worst that can happen if you ask them? They might say no or not respond. If they say yes, this gives you a great opportunity to further build your relationship. During the process, you'll get to know more about yourself and build a relationship outside of any sales conversation.

It can also be a good way to increase your reach, especially if you partner with external thought leaders with a strong network. If someone is featured in your content, they're much more likely to share it on social media with their network. Their audience then sees them promoting you and your company, naturally driving traffic and attention your way.

I often partner with external experts on my podcast, Tech Marketers Uncorked. While I host the podcast, the content is largely guest-focused and relies on external subject-matter experts to lend their expertise. Tech Marketers Uncorked starts with a wine tasting but is all about diving into the person's subject area so the audience can take away key insights and implement them into their own marketing strategy. I always learn something new every time we record. However, it also allows me to build a relationship with the people we're interviewing and then increases our reach as they help promote to their networks when the episode drops.

CREATING A CONTENT STRATEGY

Before you can consistently create thought leadership or any type of content, you'll need to define a content strategy. You want to create content regularly and ensure that every piece of content feeds into a larger marketing vision. Creating content on an ad hoc basis or using a spray-and-pray approach will not do you any favors, even if it features the best subject-matter experts.

Research shows that marketers who have a content strategy are far more likely to reach their content goals and see good results. A content strategy helps you understand the larger picture and plan so you can start creating content in advance, which makes it significantly easier to coordinate with thought leaders and internal stakeholders.

Your content strategy should set the foundation for ongoing production by helping you identify the core topics, keywords, target audience, and stages in the funnel. Essentially, your content strategy should include all the key information you need to start creating content. This also shifts some of the responsibility from your plate because if you were hit by a bus tomorrow, your team would know what content needed to be created, with whom, and by when.

Defining Content Pillars

Content pillars are essential for defining the framework of your content strategy. These are the core topics or themes that you'll build content around and should be broad enough to support multiple pieces of content. Ideally, you should be able to create at least 10 blog articles under one pillar of content. These 10 articles can then work together as part of a larger campaign to champion your expertise, increase organic search rankings, and start building a knowledge hub.

To identify your content pillars, start by asking the simple question, "*What do you want to be known for?*"

Your answer should align with your business objectives and refer back to the early positioning work as well as your customer avatars. You can build content pillars around core services, technology partners, key problems, or even topics you want to be known for, like digital innovation/transformation, customer experience, or loyalty. Once you have defined these content pillars, it's then easier to identify individual articles, SEO keywords, and types of content and build the rest of your content strategy.

SEO Keywords

You want to include SEO keywords as early as possible in your content creation process. It's much easier to bake keywords in from the beginning than to reverse-engineer content by trying to squeeze

SEO keywords into content later on in the process when content has already been written. Your keyword research might also influence the articles you create, as you may find that a large number of people are searching for a specific question or other long-tail keyword.

Start by conducting keyword research by using your content pillars as seed keywords. What terms are relevant to your audience and related to the key topics you want to be known for? What are people searching for around these seed keywords? What long-tail keywords should you create content around?

Once you have a list of potential keywords, you then want to consider search volume and keyword difficulty. Suppose you're relatively new to marketing or have a limited budget. In that case, you'll want to focus on keywords that aren't particularly difficult to rank for, as this will allow you to achieve a bigger impact quicker. You also want to pay attention to search volume as you want to create content that people are *actually* looking for. However, B2B or luxury brands might be able to choose keywords with a lower search volume (assuming the keywords are highly relevant for their brands) as they don't need a large number of leads but rather high-quality leads.

By examining keyword relevancy, search volume, and difficulty, you can choose at least one primary keyword for each standard-length article. Articles of 2,000 words or more should have at least two to three keywords.

Remember Your Audience

When you're identifying relevant keywords or article topics, it's important to remember your audience and refer back to your buyer personas. Your audience should play a leading role in deciding what type of content you'll create, on what topics, and around which keywords. After all, there's no point in creating content that your audience isn't interested in or won't find meaningful.

To ensure all the content you create remains focused on the audience, align each piece of content with one of the buyer personas and include this information in the content strategy. This ensures you never forget who you're writing for and keep them front and center throughout the process.

Ideally, you want to create at least one piece of content every month for each buyer persona. Content is essentially a conversation you're having with your audience. So, if you don't create content on a regular basis, it's the equivalent of not speaking with your audience. Furthermore, if you need to speak to each buyer persona monthly, then this will also dictate content frequency, as the more buyer personas you have, the more content you'll need to create each month.

Stages in the Funnel

As part of building a relationship with your audience, you'll also want to consider how content can support them throughout the purchasing journey. Ideally, content should nurture them from the first point of contact to final conversion. Obviously, you'll need multiple touchpoints throughout this process, but long-form content certainly plays a key role at each stage.

As such, your content strategy should feature content at each stage of the funnel:

Top of the Funnel (TOFU)

Top-of-funnel content tends to lean heaviest toward SEO as it answers some of their early questions and is designed to capture your audience's attention before they know who you are. At this stage, they're simply looking for a solution to a specific problem but aren't sure who or sometimes even what.

Longer-form content, like Ultimate Guides, works particularly well here as it casts a wider net by being more generalized and appropriate for the early research stages. Think of top-of-funnel content like a first date: What would you want someone to know about you right out of the gate?

Mid of Funnel (MOFU)

Mid-of-funnel content is slightly further along in the journey and is often where you start to get into juicier, meatier, and more personalized pieces. Thought leadership content works particularly well here as it's an opportunity to showcase your company and tell your audience more about what it's like to work with you without being sales-focused. Content at this stage should strike a balance between being informative while also allowing you to showcase a unique perspective, opinion, or expertise so you stand out from your competitors.

This is where you get into the details and allow your audience to continue their learning journey by diving beneath the surface. Think of mid-funnel content like the fifth date. This is really where you start to shine and further your relationship by letting them into your world.

Bottom of Funnel (BOFU)

Bottom-of-funnel content is much closer to conversion and, as such, acts as a way to build final credibility to get the deal over the line, like case studies or capturing your audience's details so your sales team can pick up the conversation. Case studies are one of the most effective BOFU assets as by the time someone reads your case study, they're not deciding if they need your service but whether you're the right company to help solve their problem. As such, it's a massively missed opportunity to not have case studies on your website.

Downloadable assets are one of the other most common types of BOFU content. They can either be short form like templates, checklists, or interactive quizzes or longer, meatier whitepapers and e-books featuring industry thought leaders. Since downloadable assets require your audience to enter their details, like name and email, to access the content, it's important to create assets that deliver quite a lot of value and are extremely meaningful to your audience. No one wants to download something that won't help them or isn't worth reading, and your audience is likely to feel let down or even ripped off if your content doesn't deliver.

However, done right, downloadable content can be a great way to capture key details about your audience and further the relationship. You can then use their details (especially if they opt in) to invite them to future events, send newsletters, etc.

Aligning Content Strategy with Sales

Content helps you build relationships at scale, which decreases your reliance on your sales team. Rather than needing salespeople to answer every question and be constantly available to prospects, done correctly, your content can support prospects around the clock by delivering the information they need. Content, unlike your sales team, is available 24/7, so it can be on hand to answer crucial questions at 3 in the morning or on Sunday afternoons. Aligning your content with your sales team's needs and overall strategy not only makes your sales team's jobs easier but also ensures you support your audience in the right way at the right time.

While aligning sales and marketing is important in all industries, some industries, like B2B, face extremely long sales cycles, so it's even more important to think about how you keep prospects engaged at scale and over time. If the average B2B sales cycle is 180 to 270 days, you'll need to think about the touchpoints for nurturing prospects through the funnel and ensure your content marketing strategy delivers.

When creating content to support your sales team, it can be good to sit down with a senior salesperson, like the chief revenue officer or chief growth officer, to ask some strategic questions. For example,

- What questions do they often hear from prospects?
- What are the prospect's main concerns when considering your product or service?
- Where in the sales funnel do prospects get stuck or fall out? Would having more information at this stage help?
- What sales collateral is perhaps missing, and does any new content need to be created?

These questions should help reveal important opportunities for content creation and ensure your content strategy fully supports your sales team to build relationships at scale.

Designing a Content Campaign

Content often works best when it's part of a campaign rather than an ad-hoc or sporadic approach where you might have multiple pieces of random content. Content should supercharge the results and build your expertise.

I particularly like HubSpot's content pillar campaign approach. At the top of the funnel, you create a long-form (normally 2,000-word) article that targets a high-volume keyword with a high keyword difficulty. You then create several supporting articles (around 1,000 words each) that target related long-tail keywords that leverage thought leadership and act as more mid-funnel content. At the bottom, you have either a downloadable asset like a template or checklist or an e-book/ white paper.

Each article should end with a clear call to action to download the e-book, and it must all feature links to the other articles. Internal linking is often overlooked but is important for creating structure and also telling Google the relationship between pieces of content.

As part of creating this campaign, you can also repurpose and integrate old content. I normally recommend conducting at least a light touch content audit after defining your content pillar to identify any articles that might work in the campaign. These might need to be reworked before they can be used but integrating them into the campaign provides extra umph—both because they already have some domain authority and also by allowing you to add extra strings to your bow.

Once the articles are created, it's important to think about how the content is promoted. SEO will take time to work properly, so you need to consider quicker win ways to drive traffic to the articles, such as social media and email. When I'm designing a content campaign, I also normally include a certain amount of social posts, paid LinkedIn content (if it fits within the budget), and drip emails. Content dissemination allows you to expand the reach by getting in front of your audience on channels they're already using or, as I like to say, fishing where the fish are.

This campaign works across the funnel and drives to increase your chances of securing a page-one ranking for the difficult keyword while also driving readers down the funnel and capturing their details with the BOFU asset. I've used this campaign in many of my strategies and have often seen good results.

HOW TO CREATE THOUGHT LEADERSHIP CONTENT

Creating a sound content strategy is only half the battle. Once you've set your content strategy, you then need to think about how you create the content and bring your strategy to life. You'll want to think about *who* will create the content, especially if you're creating thought leadership content, as this is one area where brands often get tripped up, as thought leaders really shouldn't create their own content.

Why Thought Leaders Shouldn't Create Their Own Content

When a brand first starts producing thought leadership content, it's quite easy to fall into the trap of having thought leaders create their own content. After all, they're the subject-matter experts, so it makes sense that the person with the knowledge or expertise would create the content. However, this often doesn't work as thought leaders struggle to find the time as they normally have day jobs outside of marketing. If they do find time to produce content, they often create content that is so technical that it doesn't resonate with your audience and goes right over their heads.

As subject-matter experts in the business, these individuals are often under pressure from many departments. They're the go-to person any time anything goes wrong and are constantly putting out fires and struggling with competing priorities. As a result, and quite rightly so, creating an article or e-book falls to the bottom of the list and simply doesn't happen.

Since they also know the subject like the back of their hand, they often lack perspective on what someone else (like your audience) does or doesn't know. Without this perspective, they then easily fall into the knowledge gap and create content that they'd like to read but may be too technical or not relevant to your audience. After all, if your audience understood your field as well as you did, they wouldn't need you.

They also don't understand marketing best practices, like how to optimize an article for SEO. If your content isn't SEO optimized, you're missing a real trick, as your content won't be working for you, and no one will find it. Articles need not only to capture thought leaders' expertise but also to meet all the best practices for SEO, mobile, and digital marketing.

Hidden Cost of Having Thought Leaders Create Their Own Content

There's also a hidden cost of having thought leaders create their own content. Most thought leaders are super seasoned and experienced individuals, which means they'll be getting a salary of over $150k (roughly $85/hour). Content takes quite a bit of time to create with most blogs taking between six to 10 hours, which suddenly puts the financial cost on par with working with an agency.

In addition, by having them focus on creating content, they're not focused on other high-priority areas of the business, like landing a new client, fixing a critical bug in the program, or nurturing a high-value client relationship. So, you also have to factor in the loss of opportunities from not having them focused on their day job.

Capturing their Expertise

So, if thought leaders shouldn't create their own content, how do you capture their expertise and create high-quality technical content? Do you need to find a copywriter who is *also* an expert in your niche area?

Many brands think that if they can't use their internal experts, they need a copywriter with the same level of expertise. For example, a copywriter with in-depth knowledge of underwriting for insurance and MGAs. However, copywriters often won't have the same level of expertise as thought leaders because if they did, they'd be underwriters earning a far higher salary.

Instead, I think the best middle ground is uniting the power of copywriting with subject-matter expertise via journalist-style interviews. Interviews only require 20 to 30 minutes of the subject-matter expert's time, but they allow you to work with a writer who understands digital marketing best practices and can translate these insights into a way your audience will understand.

While the writer needs to understand the space enough to be able to have an intelligent conversation, they don't need the same level of expertise as someone who works in your business or niche area all day, every day. Nor should they, as your audience won't have this level of understanding. Even CTOs or C-suite executives won't understand your business or product like your team.

Interviews can be a very effective way to create thought leadership content, but sometimes subject-matter experts are so busy with their day jobs that they don't have time to sit for interviews. One way around this is to repurpose previous talks, podcasts, or other mediums where they've shared their thoughts and opinions. Subject-matter experts will often appear on-stage at conferences, on podcasts, or, at the very least, give internal presentations. If you record these events, you can use the insights shared to replace the interviews and leverage these insights for content opportunities to allow you to still create thought leadership content.

Speaking to Your Audience in a Way They Understand

One of the main drawbacks to having subject-matter experts create their own content is that they often don't understand the audience and assume that everyone understands the subject to the same degree and in the same way they do. It's really easy to make this mistake when you work in the field all day, every day. You're too close to the forest to see the trees.

Conducting interviews helps shift the perspective from the subject-matter expert to the writer. Any good writer should be able to see the content from your audience's perspective and help break down terms or concepts they might not understand. Overcoming this knowledge gap is essential if you want to create content that truly speaks to your audience.

Content should be seen as a way to kick-start important conversations and build meaningful relationships. And as such, it's important to think about how you speak to your audience. What information do they need to know before they speak to someone on your team? What burning questions do they have? How can you create content that answers these questions and supports your audience around the clock?

Creating an Outline

After you've conducted an interview with a thought leader or conducted your desk research, it's important to create a detailed outline. Your outline allows you to get internal stakeholders to sign off and ensure everyone is on the same page before you dive head-first into content creation. Outlines are like the blueprint for a house; it helps avoid surprises later down the road as you know exactly what floor your bathroom will go on. Getting sign-off on your outline then helps to avoid large-scale restructuring or substantial edits, which can be costly and require extensive time to correct.

If you've conducted subject-matter expert interviews, it can be a good idea to get their feedback at this stage to ensure you're headed in the right direction. I normally, however, recommend limiting the number of internal stakeholders who feed into an outline and the article in general. Content can be very subjective, so you don't want too many cooks in the kitchen, or you can easily find yourself pulled in many different and often conflicting directions.

Outlines are also helpful from a writing perspective, as once you have an outline, it's much easier to overcome writer's block. Instead of staring at a blank page, which can be super intimidating, you have an already-approved direction to head in and simply need to fill in the blanks. Working from an outline is then like coloring in a coloring book rather than drawing a picture completely from scratch.

I've experienced the benefits of outlines firsthand, and we use this approach with almost all of our clients. We, at the very least, start any new engagement with an outline, as this helps get the relationship off on the right foot by having everyone on the same page. Sometimes, once we get up and running, we cut back on outlines to save time for our clients.

Two Sets of Eyes: Proofreading

Before you submit your article for final review with your subject-matter expert or main stakeholder, it's good to have someone else proofread it. Having two sets of eyes on a piece of content is extremely helpful. When you've spent hours working on an article, it's sometimes easy to miss simple mistakes as you see what *should* be there rather than what *is* there. This makes it extremely easy to miss typos or other small errors. That's why we always have two copywriters on a project as it allows for an additional screening and quality control before sending any content to our clients.

It also means that there's another copywriter who's fully up to speed on an account and can step in to cover any additional demand or if the other copywriter is sick or gets hit by a bus. You never want to be in a position where all the brand knowledge is locked in one person's head.

If you're a team of one and don't have someone to review your content, there are some great proofreading tools out there, like Grammarly or Hemmingway. Both can help catch some of these simple mistakes and improve your overall content.

Content Dissemination

Creating a great piece of content is only half the battle. Once you hit publish, you then need to ensure people know the content is available and can easily find it. While SEO can help drive organic traffic, especially if your article is optimized properly, SEO can also take time and isn't a quick win. However, there are some things you can do in the meantime to increase visibility and help get the word out about your content.

Any content you create should complement your other marketing efforts. Rather than thinking of content as a separate endeavor, it's helpful to think of your marketing as a whole. As we discussed previously, this is where content campaigns come into play. But even if you don't have a full content campaign, at the very least, you should promote your content asset across all your main social media channels and via email.

With social media, you want to create more than one social post. Social media channels push out content only to a select group of your connections or followers, so not all first-degree connections will see all posts, especially from a company account. I normally recommend creating at least three social media posts per blog article (more for whitepapers/e-books) and also ensuring that senior leaders and employees within the business share the content. Personal accounts perform better than company accounts, especially on LinkedIn, so it's likely that their posts will get greater traction and further reach.

Instead of having them directly re-share the content, encourage them to create unique social posts that share their thoughts or opinions on the piece. Posts that are reshared don't perform as well on the LinkedIn algorithm as unique content.

With email dissemination, you might consider including recent articles in your newsletter or creating custom drip email campaigns to support your content. Short-form blog articles tend not to carry as much importance or deliver as much value, so they are often better suited for newsletters, whereas e-books have enough value to justify a dedicated email campaign. With e-books, you can also add a graphic with a link to download to your email footer. Email footers are a great advertising space but are often overlooked or ignored entirely—certainly, a missed opportunity.

Content dissemination is important for ensuring your content performs to the best of its ability and that you're properly signposting people to your articles. After all, you can create an amazing article, but if you don't tell people it's there, no one will find it. A "build it, and they will come" mentality doesn't work with marketing.

Chapter 10

Gaining Momentum and Building a Community

As you build your brand and gain momentum, you'll naturally start to build an audience, and eventually, when this audience becomes big enough and has enough in common, you'll start to create a community. Being part of and having a community around you is massively important for accelerating your marketing and brand building. Having a community allows you to drive inbound leads, unlock new opportunities, and truly elevate brand awareness. After all, it takes a community to raise a child (or, in our world, a business).

When you start building a brand, you have to fish where the fish are by going directly to your audience. But, as your brand grows and you create a community that they want to be part of, it becomes like creating a feeding pool. All of a sudden, you have a captive audience that wants to be part of what you're creating, and it becomes much easier to elevate your brand.

Many marketers understand the power of having a community, but few have one. It's not easy to create a community around your brand, and it takes time to get proper momentum. Most marketers lose focus before they have a self-sustaining community, so many are abandoned out there. Like most marketing, it takes time and consistent effort to build a community. Doing so allows you to create brand advocates who spread the word about your company, send people your way, and attract people (partners, clients, and employees) to your business.

JOINING RELEVANT COMMUNITIES

You don't have to build a community from scratch, and often, it can be better not to, especially if there are already communities that align with your brand goals. Joining existing communities can be a great way to quickly access a network of like-minded people and begin building your audience. Many community leaders start in existing communities before branching off and creating their own, as it allows them to understand what's already out there and where the gaps may exist.

However, with communities, you get out what you put in. So, you can't simply join one and expect leads and opportunities to start flowing your way. You need to be ready to invest time, money, and resources into building your presence within the community and, perhaps most importantly, helping others.

It's significantly easier to devote your attention to a community that you already feel passionate about so try to choose a community that aligns with your interests. What makes you tick? Where do similar people hang out and spend their time? These communities are a great place to get started as you'll be surrounded by like-minded people, and investing in the community won't feel like work. Since it requires up-front investment from you, it's best to be selective with communities and what you're part of.

Once you get comfortable networking amongst your peers, it can then be helpful to think about your ideal buyer and where they spend their time. Joining these communities can be a good way to be more strategic with your efforts and increase your chances of finding new clients or partners.

When I first started growing CopyHouse, I was keen to network and reach my goal of 50 unique connections each month (see my earlier chapter on networking). So, I joined as many communities as

I could and didn't closely monitor where I was spending my time. I then realized that I was spread across several very similar communities, all catering to other agencies. While I love agencies and many of my friends run agencies, we don't work directly with agencies as most of our clients are brands. As a result, I was spending my time being part of the wrong communities that weren't necessarily going to drive revenue or leads. As such, we then became much more selective on where we were spending our time, and I then directed us towards communities that were more trade- or industry-focused since we're very niche. Or, in other words, fishing where the fish are, and we then joined communities that had more of our target brands, like Chief or The Payment Association.

SETTING THE FOUNDATIONS FOR A COMMUNITY

Once you have a strong network and followers, you can then think about creating your own community. Having your own community gives you a lot more control as you can actively shape it and have a say in its overall direction. However, having a community takes quite a lot of work, and you'll need to think about how you nurture, grow, and develop this community. Who will be part of the community, what platforms will it exist on, and how will you create a community with enough momentum to exist without you? Reaching this ultimate point will require consistent effort over a long period and certainly won't happen overnight, but the results are certainly worth pursuing.

Finding a Common Theme to Create a Community

Before you can build a community, you need to find a key theme or idea to build it around. It should be a theme or idea that people feel passionate about, so they'll actively contribute their expertise, time, and money to keep the community alive. You need to find a way to win hearts and minds, or you'll struggle to get full engagement.

One of the best ways to find this theme is to listen to your audience. What are they constantly talking about? Where do the pain points exist? And, perhaps most importantly, who needs a collective voice?

My own journey towards building a community is far from complete, but I'm building a community around tech marketers. Tech marketers are often small, one- or two-person teams that are struggling to keep their heads above water, overwhelmed with requests from other departments, and fighting against a tide of CFOs and more left-brain co-workers who don't fully understand or buy into the value of marketing. They often don't have anyone to speak with, are lonely and isolated in their departments, and need a space where they can come together. This is why my CMO roundtables are such a hit, as they bring these people together to share challenges and find solutions over something everyone can agree on—good food.

Communities can be built around any uniting theme or idea, but it's about finding the commonalities amongst your audience. Do they all enjoy a particular sport, share core values, or have the same problem? I know B2B marketers who have built communities around everything from cycling to D&I initiatives to climate change. Your options are really limitless.

Helping People

While you need a core theme or idea to build around, the main purpose of your community should be to help people and ultimately give back. A community, by its most basic definition, is a group of people who come together to beat the odds and achieve a better life, whether it's personal or professional. People need to feel that they benefit, in some shape or form, from what you're building. Perhaps the community helps them solve a specific challenge, or maybe it's more intrinsic, like making them feel less lonely. Regardless, there needs to be some feel-good elements that make people engage and continue doing so.

I love helping people; it makes me feel good, and plenty of people have taken the time to help me. I used to run a formal pay-it-forward scheme, where I donated my time to provide pro bono support to my audience. These days, we run a formal pro bono scheme to support a nonprofit that helps increase literacy rates in low-income housing estates. Giving back to your audience, as well as the wider world, should be at the forefront of your community.

Identify Collaborations and Partnerships

There's power in numbers. When you start building a community, it's helpful to think about who might be some of the early members or even partners and collaborators. Pairing up with another brand can maximize your impact as you can bring both your existing audiences together to create a much bigger community. Partners can take many forms and might be existing suppliers, other companies that sell different services to the same audience, technology platforms you build or work from, or other brands with similar interests.

These partnerships help you do more with less. For example, by partnering with another brand on an event, you can share costs, increase attendance by marketing to two different pools, and divide the man-hours required for organizing and launching the event. As your community grows, these partnerships may start to take on more of a sponsorship approach where brands pay to advertise to your audience but don't actively help or organize the event.

I think I originally approached this the wrong way around when building my audience. When we started to actively build a community via events and our podcast, I didn't initially consider partnerships as I had a strong network that I didn't *technically* need to have enough people attend our events. With my network, I could easily get over 50 people to one of our panel Tech Talk events. It wasn't until we started to exceed our internal resources (both in regard to our marketing manager's time and budget) that I realized I had missed a trick. We also had the additional complication of needing to build a new audience in a new market with our expansion into the US. Partnerships then offered a way to do more with less (or the same) while also tapping into a new audience. I wish I had focused more on partnerships earlier in the journey, as this would have certainly made our lives easier.

Community Leaders: Having a Front-Runner

Most communities have front-runners, at least at the beginning, who can be the main relationship holders and bring people into the events. This person hosts events, keeps the WhatsApp groups or Slack communities active, and ensures the momentum continues, even when others are tired or aren't as active. They constantly have new ideas about how to grow the community and engage existing members, and they are, in other words, the lifeblood.

Ideally, you want someone who has a strong personal brand, is naturally extroverted, and enjoys being the life of the party. They'll need to play host while also taking time out to help other members and effectively put their arms around people.

Normally, this might be the company founder or a senior leader as they may already have existing networks and are used to inspiring people to be part of their journey. All companies have front-runners who inspire people to be part of their journey, but normally, this is only directed at employees rather than a wider audience. Flipped externally, this ability to inspire becomes particularly powerful.

As the community grows and members take a more active role, this community leader may not be relied on as heavily and may start to become more of a figurehead. When other members start to encourage engagement and help each other, new members are recruited without the leader's involvement, and the WhatsApp groups are active without any help, then you'll have enough momentum for the community leader not to need to be as actively involved. At this stage, they may start to focus more on event appearances and promoting the community on a larger stage.

Exclusivity or Not

Some communities are incredibly exclusive as to the people they let become members. I'm a member of some of these communities. However, I'm not a big fan of exclusive communities as they often overlook a key part of a marketing strategy—brand advocates. Someone may not meet the criteria for being a member but could be a massive advocate for your brand and ultimately send more opportunities your way than a full-fledged community member. Brand advocates are often overlooked because they don't fit the ideal buyer persona but are underestimated in the power they can bring to your organization.

Often, the best approach is to take a dual approach, where some events are more exclusive, and others are open to everyone. This allows you to create a community where no one is left out, and everyone can engage in some way. By allowing everyone to engage, you don't risk alienating brand advocates or people who refer business to you.

I'm personally a big fan of making everyone feel welcome as I've been excluded before, especially at school when I was younger, and it's really not a nice feeling. I make my community as inclusive as possible by providing different experiences for different audience subsets. We host a CMO roundtable that's invite-only and geared toward brand CMOs, while our panel-style Tech Talk events are open to everyone, and my podcast, Tech Marketers Uncorked, is free to download from Spotify. I've certainly seen the power of brand advocates with this approach, as we've had people who attend our Tech Talks and wouldn't qualify as our ideal buyer persona or receive an invite for the CMO Tech Talk to refer work to. I also feel better about myself by creating something that everyone can be a part of.

ACTIVATION: HOW TO BUILD A COMMUNITY

Once you have the idea, audience, and leader for your community, the next step is to decide on the main channels and platforms. How will you actually build your community? What techniques will you use to bring and keep members together?

Keep It Simple

Initially, I recommend choosing one core platform on which to build a community. Communities don't need to be overly complicated, and I know plenty of brilliant communities that were originally built only via WhatsApp, Slack, newsletters, or even podcasts. You need a communication platform where your audience can engage with one another and you as the brand. In essence, it's all about creating and facilitating conversations.

As you grow, you might expand efforts to start including other channels and platforms, including in-person or online events. Since it takes quite a lot of consistent effort to build a community, I recommend starting simple and not biting off more than you can chew. Take it one platform or channel at a time, so once you have an active, self-sustaining WhatsApp group, add a podcast or in-person events, and so forth. This gradual rollout ensures you don't spread yourself too thin and have enough resources to dedicate to properly building your community and sustaining momentum.

In-Person and Online Events

I'm a big believer in events. While I know that communities can be built on other platforms, there's something special about coming together in person with people and being able to connect in real life. It isn't easy to replace or replicate this online.

However, in-person events are also problematic, especially if you're trying to reach a more global audience. In-person events, by their very nature, are both time- and location-restrictive, so people may not be able to engage in the community if they don't live in one location. My attitude toward in-person events is a reaction to not being able to spend time with people in person, which, as an extrovert, was very anxiety-producing. My mental health was at an all-time low during the pandemic, mostly because I couldn't spend time with other people.

Now, with some perspective, I can see the benefits of online and in-person events and believe the best strategy is a healthy combination of the two. Online events allow you to reach a wider, more geographically diverse audience, which extends your reach. However, they also have a high dropout rate, so they need to be massively oversubscribed to ensure adequate attendance. It's much easier for people not to attend when their physical environment, like co-workers or the comfy couch, is competing for their time and attention.

Nonetheless, events are an important part of community building as they give you the opportunity to bring people together and create shared experiences. Memories are one of the core, fundamental ways that we bond with others and create deeper relationships, which are required for creating enough connections across the community so that it becomes self-sustaining. I love it when I hear about some of the connections or opportunities that happen for people who attend our events or are part of our community. Hearing that they met someone and they then went for a coffee, and that created a new opportunity is one of my favorite things.

Podcasting

Building a community requires devotion. You have to be willing to give and help an audience that may never return the favor. It's this act of putting yourself forward and opening your heart (or mind) that allows a community to start to form.

One common way of giving to your community is by creating a podcast as part of your community-building efforts. The podcast allows you to share your expertise and give free advice to help listeners learn something new or solve a particular challenge. For example, my podcast, Tech Marketers Uncorked, is all about digging into the guests' expertise and pulling out key insights that listeners can then use to build their own marketing strategies. Creating this podcast is super time-consuming and expensive, and I may never see any results or even know who's listened to it. But if my podcast can help one tech marketer feel less lonely, then it's done its job.

While podcasts certainly have trackable metrics, most podcasts are very top-of-the-funnel, which means that it's difficult to track the exact return on your investment. However, by listening to your episodes, your audience starts to get to know you better and builds a connection that makes them far more likely to want to come to your events or be part of the community.

WhatsApp/Slack Groups

Almost all communities have a WhatsApp or Slack group. These channels help members connect and engage with one another, often without the leaders' help. They're great places for asking questions, sharing interesting ideas, and arranging to meet up/get together. However, they can be difficult to maintain, and I find the information I receive from them to be overwhelming at times.

Admittedly, I haven't started my own WhatsApp group because of these drawbacks, but it's something I'm considering as it allows people in the community to connect on their own accord and contributes toward creating a self-sustaining community, which, after all, is the ultimate goal.

REACHING THE FINAL DESTINATION: CREATING A SELF-SUSTAINING COMMUNITY

I've talked a lot about the self-sustaining community and this is truly the point you want to get to if you're building a community. A self-sustaining community becomes bigger than the brand or community leader and starts to take on a life of its own. It starts to have its own set of values and identity so it actually means something to members to be part of that community.

When you reach this point, members are much more connected and are all pulling together behind one common cause. Even if you didn't organize events or post in the WhatsApp group, conversations and meetings would continue. If the community leader dropped out, a new one would be found.

This is community nirvana, and few brands reach this stage, either because the idea never had enough legs, not enough resources (be it time or money) were invested, or the community leader withdrew before the community could stand on its own. Creating a community is a bit like raising a child, and it needs to reach a certain level of maturity before resources can be withdrawn or the community leader can stop being active. Lose them too early or not put enough into the community, and like a plant, it'll wither and die.

It's really important to properly consider the long-term vision and strategy before starting to build a community. You'll need patience and enough resources to be able to get it off the ground, and anything less won't suffice. But get it right, and having a community will pay dividends. After all, I'm a big believer that a brand is what people say about you when you're not in the room.

Chapter 11

Growing Your Brand Internationally

Once you start to gain brand awareness and momentum, you may consider expanding internationally. This offers quite a few strategic advantages as it allows you to tap into new markets, serve a new customer base, and diversify risk.

I know I've always been attracted to international markets. Not only do I love traveling, but we've always had at least some international clients. At first, our focus was on the European market, as 10 percent of our audience was here in the UK, but over the last few years, it's become much more US-focused. I've learned a few lessons while expanding internationally, but perhaps most importantly, I've learned how difficult expanding globally and maintaining momentum is on the world stage. Expanding globally is much harder than you think.

When I set up CopyHouse, I had been a freelance copywriter for about a year or so and some of my early clients were based in Europe. However, I saw the potential for us in the European market, and after a few years of building the CopyHouse brand, I started to think about expanding internationally more seriously. Since we specialize in content marketing for technology brands, we have a limited pool of relevant clients in the UK. If we were then going to stay focused on this niche, we needed to find a way to increase our client pool, and international expansion offered one solution.

One of my first moves to establish CopyHouse in Europe was to formally set up a European company. However, I soon discovered that establishing and owning an international business presented some unforeseen challenges. For example, at the time, there was a real talent shortage in the UK and I had seen international expansion as a way to hire globally and access talented candidates. I had assumed that establishing an EU company would allow me to do so. However, European companies can only hire within the country they're established in and can't hire across the whole EU.

While there were some legal complications, we also didn't design or implement a designed marketing strategy for the EU market. We assumed that our marketing for the UK would help us attract clients in the EU and didn't create a separate budget or strategy for it. Some digital marketing can work across borders, but you also need marketing activations that are targeted specifically for that market. As a result, our expansion into Europe never really gained enough traction and gradually died off, which I think is quite common for most brands that attempt to expand internationally.

It's easy to underestimate cultural differences when entering a new market and not dedicate enough resources to fully launching your company or assume that the marketing campaigns you're running in one country will help you attract clients in another. Without a designed strategy and budget, for that matter, it's almost impossible to gain traction in a new market. Expanding globally shouldn't be taken lightly, and if you really want to expand into a new market, it's important to know what you're getting into and how you can make it a success.

WHERE MOST BRANDS GO WRONG WITH INTERNATIONAL EXPANSION

Many brands try to take what they've done in one market and quite literally lift and shift it into another market without any consideration for cultural differences or even realizing that they don't have the same brand credibility and awareness in this new market. I've seen far too many brands make this mistake. One message that I want to make very clear is that *What works in one market doesn't necessarily work in another,* and this 'lift and shift' approach almost never works.

Take, for example, the recent closure of Chief UK.

Chief is well-known in the US with a waitlist of over 60,000 people. Last year, they decided to expand into the UK and capitalize on their US success in the European market. However, the club wasn't known in the UK or Europe and made almost no marketing efforts to build brand awareness in a new market. Within a year of opening in the UK, they had to close their doors and retreat back to the US. Recent news articles have claimed that their closure was due to a lack of demand from female executives, but as almost all marketers know, demand comes from marketing, and without proper marketing, there is no demand. It's not due to a lack of interest but by assuming that their success in the US would naturally translate to the UK, and they didn't need to do any additional marketing to raise brand awareness.

I meet many brands that make this mistake as they attempt to take an existing strategy into a new market. However, new markets require a new approach (both with marketing and the wider business). Certain techniques, channels, and even messaging resonate very differently depending on the market. For example, Facebook is still massively popular in Asia and Africa with many businesses only having a Facebook Business Page rather than an actual website. However, Facebook is largely dead in the UK and the US (apart from paid advertising, of course). Likewise, webinars work much better in the US, where teams are spread across the States and used to attending online sessions, compared to the UK, where everyone is based in London and can quite easily attend in-person events.

As such, it's important to start with a blank sheet when building your international strategy. Sure, some elements of your existing strategy might work globally, but you want to avoid making assumptions and ensure you take a fresh, market-relevant approach to your strategy.

Problem with US-Centric Marketing in International Expansion

Most big brands are headquartered in the US and over the last few years, as brands have tried to do more with less, there's been a movement to consolidate marketing into the US. This means that US-based teams are left running all global marketing efforts, and while this may seem logical to some, it becomes problematic when US teams either assume that everything outside of the States is *global* or don't consider the cultural connotations. This is even more common than when it comes to expanding into the UK market.

I grew up in the US and didn't move to the UK till my early 20s, so I'm perhaps particularly well-suited to comment on the cultural differences between the US and the UK. While the countries may share what appears to be a similar language, the psyche, mentality, and attitudes could not be more different. The old saying "two countries separated by a common language" certainly applies here.

Utimately, marketing is all about understanding your audience intimately and creating campaigns that resonate with them. It's nearly impossible to achieve this without understanding their culture and lived experiences. However, all hope is not lost, as there are certainly ways American-based marketing teams can ensure they don't create marketing campaigns without cultural resonance.

One of the best ways is to live in or visit your target countries. Spending time on the ground allows you to get to know your market, local attitudes, and psyche and begin to see how you might create marketing that resonates with them. If you're not able to travel there, at the very least, spend time speaking with co-workers who are there.

It's important for any marketing team creating global content to first recognize the weight of cultural differences and remember that approaches that work in your country may not work elsewhere.

DECIDING YOUR INTERNATIONAL MARKETS

Before you can expand internationally or begin to build a global marketing strategy, you'll need to decide on your target markets and where you'll focus your attention. I recommend choosing one market and getting your marketing up and running before expanding further. You, ideally, want to avoid biting off more than you can chew. While you can try to launch in multiple markets at once, you will need more resources, including budget and people, to do this successfully, as otherwise, you may find that you're stretched too thin to have the desired results.

Choosing your focus markets may be a decision that's made at the board or executive level. If they're smart, they should ask for your feedback on markets, as marketers often have a better understanding of your audience than those at the board level. You should be able to advise on where you have the most traction. It always makes sense to build on your existing customer and audience base, so one of the best ways to decide on target markets is to look at your databases. Your marketing database will contain lots of useful information about where you have connections, partners, and perhaps already existing customers. These connections will make your life significantly easier as you won't need to build entirely from scratch but will have people who can introduce you to others, open doors, or help direct you.

You may also want to consider some of the more practical limitations. For example, how far away is your target market (do you have anyone who is either happy to relocate to give you boots on the ground or easily travel there), and are there financial considerations like taxes, exchange rates, or regulatory restrictions? Speaking to an international business advisor can be helpful for some of the legal or financial challenges that center on expanding into a new market and potentially establishing a new business there or securing any required licenses.

DEFINING YOUR INTERNATIONAL MARKETING STRATEGY

Once you've decided on your target market, you can then start build-ing your international marketing strategy. As we touched on earlier, it's often best to take a fresh approach to your international marketing strategy, as creating an entirely new strategy helps you avoid the 'lift and shift' approach and ensures everything you do is done with your new audience in mind. Of course, some of the techniques you cur-rently use and find successful will work here, too, but it's best to avoid making assumptions. As my mother used to say, "When you assume, you make an ass out of you and me."

Start the process of building your international marketing strategy by studying the foundations of your original strategy through market research, competitor analysis, and ideal buyer personas.

Market Research

You'll want to begin by conducting extensive market research and hopefully even spend some time on the ground getting to know your new market. Some subtle cultural references are difficult to understand without visiting the country and truly absorbing the culture. However, I also realize that spending long periods on the ground may not nec-essarily be possible for your entire team, and that's okay.

If you can't spend time on the ground, speak to as many people as you can about life there. You ultimately want to understand what it's like to be in your target buyer's shoes and their lived experiences within that country. What cultural connotations need to be taken into consideration? How do they prefer to engage with brands?

The more people you can speak to with experience in these mar-kets, the better. You might want to speak to co-workers, existing cus-tomers, or even network connections who work and live in these markets. These conversations will help you paint a picture of your target market and ensure that the decisions you make when imple-menting a marketing campaign align accordingly.

Resetting Your Buyer Personas

As part of setting the foundations for your marketing strategy, it's important to take a look at your existing buyer personas. Hopefully, you already have buyer personas for your home market, but you'll want to reset these to ensure they're still relevant for your target market. Are you targeting the same audience? If so, do they have the same pain points and challenges in the new market? How might their lives or roles differ in the new market? Do they prefer to engage with brands via a different platform or style than in your home market? And, perhaps more fundamentally, what do they ultimately need from your brand?

It can be helpful to re-run the buyer persona workshop to ensure that you have fresh personas for your international marketing strategy and that any cultural differences are considered. It's very unlikely that your existing buyer personas are entirely the same in a new market.

Competitor Analysis

Similarly to resetting your buyer personas, you also want to understand your new market and the competitors that play in that space. How do they differ from your home market competitors? How do they position themselves, and how do they talk about their services? Looking at how they position themselves can tell you a lot about the market and ensures that your USPs are not only relevant but still a competitive advantage.

You can also learn a lot about the marketing approaches that work in your new market. What platforms are these competitors active on? What techniques or approaches are they using and how do these differ from the approaches that work in your market?

Looking at your competitors is massively helpful for understanding what works well, what they're not doing so well, and how you can gain a competitive advantage to gain market traction in your new target country.

Creating a Global Market Strategy: Market Specific vs Shared-Resource

Once you've set the foundations by re-examining and defining your buyer personas and conducting a competitor analysis, you can start to think about and map out your marketing strategy. Generally, there are two types of approaches to creating a global marketing strategy, and the one you choose will depend on your budget, desire to expand and how serious you are about establishing yourself in this new market.

Market-Specific Strategy

One approach, and perhaps the gold standard, is to create a market-specific strategy that is unique and zeroed into each target market. This allows you to ensure that all assets are entirely personalized and extremely relevant for the market, which then helps you to establish yourself quicker as there's no mistaking that you're a serious player and are 100 percent aligned with that market. However, this approach requires more budget and resources to implement. Ideally, you'll have a separate budget for each market with a dedicated team to implement the strategy.

If you take this approach, you'll want to ensure that you have an overarching strategy that ties all the individual markets together. Without this overarching strategy, it can be easy for there to be waste as different markets aren't working together and don't know what the other markets are doing. As a result, elements of the campaign that could be used in other markets aren't and you can quite easily end up with duplication or excess spending. The left hand needs to know what the right hand is doing.

Syncing all market specific strategies into one larger strategy helps ensure all teams stay on the same page and aren't undertaking activities that could either be shared or adjusted. After all, you need everyone working together, even if they're ultimately serving different markets, and silos are never good in marketing.

Shared-Resource Global Marketing Strategy

If you don't have the budget, resources, or desire to create market-specific strategies, you can take a more generalized approach by creating one global marketing strategy. This allows you to share resources and, in some ways, work more efficiently. However, designing a shared-resource global marketing strategy that resonates with all audiences is no easy task, and it will likely resonate more with one market than another.

To strike the right balance and achieve the best results with a shared-resource global marketing strategy, you need to find the common threads between your markets. What topics or narratives would work within all the markets? These pillars can then serve as the base of your campaign and allow you to create marketing collateral that only needs to be adjusted slightly to be relevant to the market. So, instead of creating a piece 100 percent from scratch, you can adjust 20 percent of the content by ensuring it includes the right language, stats, and examples from the market. However, in order to do this successfully, you need to be able to ensure the general gist of the campaign is relevant and valuable for each market.

Creating campaigns that work across markets requires very strong foundations, as it's easy to create content that's tone-deaf or not market-relevant. This often results in campaigns that either don't work or, worst case, are considered offensive within the market. So, while it's certainly possible to design campaigns that work across markets and only require a few tweaks, it's best to proceed with caution and ensure you still have a good understanding of your target markets.

IMPLEMENTING A GLOBAL MARKETING STRATEGY

Once you have designed your marketing campaign, either for market-specific or shared resources, taking cultural implications into account, you can then start to implement your marketing strategy.

Implementing a global marketing strategy requires more resources and budget than focusing only on one market so you'll need to account for this. You'll also need to be patient, as it will take time to build brand awareness in your new market. Typically, brand awareness takes six to 12 months, depending on market saturation and how much resources you're able to invest to get it up and running quickly.

Setting a Budget

Perhaps one of the biggest mistakes brands make when expanding internationally is not assigning a new budget. You'll need a bigger budget and more resources to successfully enter a new market and build brand awareness. Even if you're taking a shared-resource approach, you may be able to replicate some of your efforts in the new market, but you'll still need to personalize content and campaigns to ensure they're relevant to your new market. As such, it's important to set a defined budget for your new target market and each market should really have its own budget.

When determining your budget, it's important to consider the exchange rates and average costs within your target market. Sometimes, activities in one country will cost significantly more than in another. This can apply to paid advertising, for example, but it can also apply to conferences, events, and sponsorships. As such, try to source local quotes as much as possible.

Sourcing Suppliers

You'll likely need to partner with suppliers in your new target market to activate elements of your marketing strategy. When choosing suppliers, it's good to work with suppliers who are local and understand the market. If they're working with many brands in that country, then they'll have a good understanding of what works, what doesn't, and how you might need to adjust your approach to accommodate for cultural differences. Hopefully, they should also be able to make sure you don't launch a campaign that is offensive or doesn't translate well.

Since this is a new market, it's likely that what you pay suppliers in your home country won't be the same in a new country. Market factors, like salaries and overhead, might mean that costs are significantly higher or, if you're lucky, lower. Try to source at least a few quotes to ensure you aren't getting ripped off and can find the best value for your money.

Some services, especially digital, can also be delivered by suppliers who don't have a permanent presence in that market. For example, marketing agencies typically charge higher fees in the US, as salaries are significantly higher than those in the UK. UK-based agencies can then offer more competitive rates. However, if you go down this route, it's important to find a supplier who understands your target market and can provide practical support and knowledge on cultural differences.

Establishing Your Brand Awareness in a New Market

After you've set your budget and found the right suppliers, it's time to get practical and start implementing your marketing strategy. Remember that creating brand awareness in a new market takes time, but there are some clever ways to speed up this process and establish yourself in a new market.

Leveraging Partnerships

Similar to building your brand awareness in your home market, you need to create an audience around you in your target market. The quicker you can build a strong audience, the sooner you'll be able to produce results and drive bottom-line revenue. Building strong partnerships with brands that already have an audience in this market is a great way to do this.

You ideally want to partner with brands that already have a strong audience in the UK and are recognized as local brands. Typically, they should be companies that cater to a similar audience but offer different services. Sometimes, you may already have a relationship with these brands before you expand into the market, or you can reach out and establish them once you've selected your market. Government bodies focused on export and international expansion, like the Department of International Trade, also can help facilitate these relationships.

Once you have your partnerships, you need to co-create marketing activities to help introduce you to their audience (and vice versa) without going for the hard sell. For example, co-hosting an event allows them to introduce you to their audience and makes it easier to start building relationships around your brand.

By partnering with a company that's already established in the market, you'll essentially be able to piggyback on their market presence and brand awareness and elevate your own brand. However, remember that a good partnership is a two-way street, so you'll need to think about what you can offer your partner in return.

Joining Existing Communities

Another great way to quickly build your audience is by joining existing communities. It's likely that communities with your target audience already exist in your new target market. Becoming an active member of these communities allows you to tap into a relevant customer base and start building your network.

Creating an audience can be particularly challenging if you don't already have contacts within the market. But by joining already existing communities, you can promote your marketing activities like upcoming events and relevant thought leadership content or put a call out for guests for your podcast—essentially allowing you to hijack the community's audience and help make it your own.

To find the right community, you'll need to have a good understanding of your ideal buyer persona, who they are, and where they spend their time. It could be as simple as joining a community that targets CMOs, or you may need to be more creative by focusing on shared hobbies like triathlons or taking an industry approach. You may also already be part of communities that operate within your target market; tapping into these allows you to build on relationships you already have but with a renewed focus on a specific market.

Digital Content

In some ways, digital content knows no bounds. It can be available online to your target audience regardless of time zone and without having a physical presence. However, it's important to create digital content that's relevant to your target market, and this often requires more than simply swapping s's for z's or vice versa.

SEO

Unsurprisingly, people search for things differently in different countries. Even when they speak the same (or similar) language, how they search the Internet varies, and so does the data behind search terms. They might use specific terms, jargon, or even slang in some markets that they don't use in others.

As such, it's always worthwhile creating a separate SEO keyword strategy for each market and ensuring that any content is optimized correctly. I normally recommend optimizing for your primary market, but you may also create specific pieces of content for specific markets, and in that case, it's worth optimizing accordingly. You want to ensure your digital content works as hard for you as it can, and SEO goes a long way toward achieving this.

Stats, Figures, and Examples

If you're creating content to appeal to a global audience, it's important to use stats, figures, and examples that everyone can relate to. There are two approaches to achieving this. You can create one piece of content geared toward a global audience or update the content asset to be relevant in each market.

With one piece of content, you want to keep the stats, figures, and examples as universal as possible. For example, using USD tends to be a currency that most countries understand instead of using GBP, which is less common. However, that said, if your main headquarters are in the UK, then asking readers to convert their home currency into GBP (at least mentally) might make sense. You'll also want to think about how the examples might translate globally: Are they relevant to people who don't live in a certain country? Would there be more relevant examples that could apply to all readers? Creating an article that is relevant across the board requires strategic thought and planning.

On the other hand, it's often a good idea to update the content to be relevant to each target market. In this case, you could create a standard article like "The Ultimate Guide to Relocation" with general advice that applies to everyone. You'll then only need to update 20 to 30 percent of the article to be relevant to your target audience, so the article becomes "The Ultimate Guide to Relocating to the USA," and all stats, figures, and examples are relevant for that market.

Translation vs. Transcreation

If your target market doesn't speak English as a primary language, then you'll also need to think about translating and transcreating content. While many people speak English, if you want to connect with your target audience, it's important to offer content in their language, and Google Translate certainly won't cut it. Language is super complex and the same (or similar) language can change drastically based on regional differences as well as between different countries. So, it's extremely important to use native speakers who have on-the-ground experience and understand the subtleties of the language.

I often meet companies that attempt to have their translations done in-house by any team member who speaks the language. This can mean that Patricia from HR gets translation requests for marketing or sales collateral! As marketers, we know that this isn't ideal, as the people doing the translation should know not only the language but also how to apply it in a marketing context (i.e., optimizing for SEO, speaking to the target audience in a way the audience can understand, etc.).

Social Channels

Social media can be a bit of a different beast when it comes to creating global content as it's shorter-form content, and you have less control over the algorithm. You can't segment your audience and send specific content to specific audiences but are at the mercy of the algorithm when it comes to who sees your content, and getting engagement impacts its overall performance. So, how do you address the fact that you'll have followers from many different countries in your network? Do you create content in English or other languages?

I normally recommend that most brands use the language that the largest subset of their audience will understand. Since the algorithm will deliver the content to your first-degree connections, this increases your odds of serving content that resonates with and engages them. While this will probably be English for most brands, it also may not be. However, regardless of the exact language, you can also create content about working and operating in different markets and ensure that you create a well-rounded mix of content that tells your story.

STAYING FOCUSED & MAINTAINING MOMENTUM

Once you have your marketing strategy underway, one of the biggest challenges to expanding internationally is maintaining your momentum and staying focused. In the beginning, it will be very exciting to expand into a new market and reach a new audience. However, as with all marketing activities, it takes time to build proper momentum and start seeing the return on your efforts.

During this time, it can be very easy to lose focus, stop marketing, and essentially stop creating demand. If you don't keep the demand generation going, you'll quickly lose brand awareness. I often see the beginning of marketing as building a snowball. You pack the snowball at the top of a hill and push it down. As it goes down, it starts to get bigger and bigger until it can roll on its own. However, if you stop pushing too soon, your snowball will remain static and won't continue to grow. So, once you've started investing in a new market, ensure you stay focused and take a long-term view to gaining momentum.

Chapter 12

Tracking and Measuring Results

As any marketer can tell you, it's notoriously hard to track and measure *all* marketing results. Not only are there thousands of metrics, but the complexities of the buyer journey mean that there are many touchpoints between when someone first hears of your brand and when they convert, and not all these touchpoints are measurable (like word of mouth). Identifying, defining, and measuring KPIs used to be one of my least favorite parts of marketing, but as I've gained more experience and built my career, I've come to learn the importance and have witnessed firsthand the difference it can make. While it can seem intimidating at first, done right, it can mean the difference between securing and not securing a budget, or in some organizations, the difference between keeping your job or becoming redundant.

WHY RESULTS ARE IMPORTANT

You need to know where you've come from to know where you're going and the same is true with measuring results. Your metrics help you understand whether your marketing is working or whether you need to adjust your approach. They also help you get buy-in from across the organization, especially those more risk-averse roles like the CFO.

When I work with a consulting client, especially on a more long-term basis, I am constantly banging the results drum. Every time something of note happens, we secure a new SEO ranking or a piece of content attracts one of our ideal clients, I share this information with my consulting client. Of course, results are presented quarterly at board meetings in a much more formal way, but sharing wins between board meetings is a great way to build trust, reassure them that marketing is on track, and with enough good results, helps to secure more budget for activations.

While most marketers understand the importance of results, actually identifying what metrics should be tracked is much more up for debate. There are thousands of different metrics that could be tracked in marketing, and settling on the most important metrics for your brand isn't easy.

MARKETING TAKES TIME

Before you can set your KPIs or really do any marketing, it's important to understand that marketing takes time, and there aren't many quick wins. One of the biggest mistakes I see marketers, perhaps especially founders, make is to change course too quickly because they get impatient that they don't see an immediate impact on the bottom line.

I made this mistake with our first marketing hire. I knew that marketing was important but didn't fully understand how long it would take to start achieving results, and I'm definitely not known for my patience. So, about three months after making our first marketing hire, I was frustrated and impatient that we didn't have leads coming in and started to put pressure on our marketing manager to drive results quicker. However, building a brand, almost like baking a cake, isn't something you can necessarily speed up without significantly increasing the budget or internal resources, which, as a small brand, wasn't something we could do. So, I, as a founder, was putting pressure on our new marketing manager but not giving them the resources or, most importantly, time to actually achieve results, and this ultimately caused them to find a job elsewhere. While it gave us a chance to reset and rehire, I definitely didn't handle this situation correctly.

Marketing takes time. If you're building a brand from scratch, you're unlikely to see a tangible impact on the bottom line for at least six months, if not longer, and putting pressure on your marketing team to deliver results quicker will only make them look for another role elsewhere.

Instead, it's best to see marketing, especially brand building, as a long game—a game that's never over—and set KPIs across the funnel to ensure you capture low-hanging fruit for quick (or quicker) wins and invest in the brand's future.

How Long Does Marketing Take?

Marketing takes as long as it takes, and it's almost never possible to really fast-forward this. Sure, there are things you can do to speed up the process, but it only helps accelerate it to a degree. You're never going to have an overnight sensation, as most overnight sensations have years of setbacks and hard work before they go viral.

However, telling your CFO that it takes as long as it takes is not an acceptable answer, and it isn't easy to manage expectations without a clear answer. So, when pressed for timelines, I almost always start by looking at the time to close. How long does it take for the sales team to close a deal once a prospect gets in touch? Is it six months, 12, or even longer? Most B2B companies have a six-to-12-month sales cycle, but this can be longer or shorter, depending on the industry.

The average length of the sales cycle or time to close is your friend in determining how long it'll take for marketing to "work." If it takes 12 months for a deal to close, this means that the deals that are closing right now, today, were the result of activities the company took 12 months ago. So, any change to your approach or marketing needs at least this length of time to work its way through the funnel and impact revenue.

This is often the problem with chopping and changing too quickly. If your sales cycle is 12 months but you only give a new approach two to three months, then, of course, you won't see an impact on the bottom line. Clearly, you haven't given the marketing approach enough time to work.

However, waiting and being patient, especially if you are spending or investing quite a lot in a certain activity, can be very difficult. That's why it's always a good idea to set metrics across the funnel. So, how can you identify if a new activity is starting to work before it has tangible impacts on the bottom line? For example, looking at increased followers or engagement on social media is an early sign that those activities are headed in the right direction.

SETTING METRICS ACROSS THE FUNNEL

I meet many marketing teams that only track bottom-of-funnel metrics, like MQLs or SQLs. This normally happens because the sales team has set the metrics. Sales teams often have a much shorter focus than marketing or brand teams, which is the nature of their role. They're trying to hit monthly or quarterly targets, and very few think further than a quarter ahead.

Marketing activations, especially those geared toward building brand awareness, take longer than a quarter to work. Building my personal brand to over 14,000 followers and regular leads has taken five years and there's still loads of work to be done. So, focusing only on a quarter basis not only doesn't give the marketing team enough time to work but also massively tips the metrics towards the bottom-of-funnel KPIs, like MQLs.

However, to secure MQLs, especially high-quality MQLs, you need to be working across the top and middle of the funnel. The top and middle play an important part in reaching your audience, raising awareness, and getting them ready to finally convert. Without this warm-up, they'll never be ready to convert. It's like asking a random stranger if they'll marry you it's very unlikely that they'll say yes, and I have real concerns about anyone who does. To get someone to marry you, you need to court them first and build this relationship to the point that saying yes is the most natural thing in the world.

In the context of marketing, this means having enough activity and focusing on the top and mid of the funnel so that you have enough prospects at the bottom of the funnel to impact the bottom line. All funnels have churn, and while you can tighten this up with a strong understanding of your audience and ideal buyer, it's nearly impossible to eradicate. It would be like every first date turning into a second or third—it just doesn't happen. So, as a result, this means you need to understand the amount of activity required at each stage and how you'll track these results to ensure you can achieve the bottom-of-funnel results like MQLs or increases in revenue.

ALIGNING KPIS WITH YOUR COMPANY

The KPIs you choose will depend on several factors, such as the larger company objectives, stakeholder expectations, and, of course, budget.

Company/Campaign Objectives

What are you trying to achieve with your marketing? Fundamentally, marketing objectives are rather similar across the board, as almost all marketing is undertaken to increase brand awareness and market traction to drive leads. However, the finer details can change, for example, to increase brand awareness in a new market or industry or around a certain product. You might also be dealing with new circumstances or challenges like adapting to market change or merging two brand identities before you can build brand awareness. But, regardless, it's important to understand the nuances of the situation before you can determine the KPIs that will move the needle and that stakeholders care most about.

Stakeholder Expectations

Ideally, you'll be presenting these results to the board on a regular basis, so it's important to understand the metrics your stakeholders want to see most. While boards tend to want to understand campaign effectiveness and, ultimately, whether the money being spent is delivering a return on investment, including top and mid-funnel metrics on board reports is a good way to start to educate stakeholders on the importance of these activities. It's also a good idea to align the marketing metrics with wider company KPIs like an increase in revenue, market traction for expanding internationally, or other elements of the larger company strategy.

Budget

While in a dream world, KPIs wouldn't depend on a budget. It's almost impossible to separate the budget from the results. The more budget you have, the more you can achieve amazing results but the same is also true. You can't be expected to achieve big results without the right resources. I'm always very careful about creating a strategy or determining KPIs without a clear budget as it becomes far too easy to overpromise and underdeliver, which then impacts your ability to secure future budgets and could potentially put your job at risk. Instead, it's much better to take a realistic approach and identify a marketing strategy that fits within a designated budget and delivers the corresponding results.

Overpromising and Under Delivering

One of the biggest mistakes a marketer can make is to overpromise and under deliver. I think this quite easily happens when there's not a clear budget or expectations. I often met marketers who've been told by the CFO and CEO that the sky's the limit, but this is almost never true. All brands have constraints and limitations, so the sky is never truly the limit. In fact, I think this lack of direction happens because the CEO doesn't understand marketing, and the marketing manager is too junior to properly guide them to a more reasonable answer. This is where having an external consultant's advice on setting the initial strategy is really valuable.

When you clearly understand the company's larger strategy and have defined resources (budget and people), it becomes much easier to create an achievable marketing strategy and set realistic KPIs so you can overdeliver.

HOW TO SET KPIS

Setting KPIs is perhaps one of the most important parts of creating a marketing strategy. These will allow you to set and manage expectations, advocate for your work, and ultimately help you unlock more budget so you can do more. That might feel like a lot of pressure, but it doesn't have to be as scary!

Step #1: Review Objectives

Before I create a marketing strategy, I always review the wider company objectives as well as the constraints. You want to have a clear idea of the company strategy, available resources (budget and people), and, ideally, what stakeholders would like to achieve before you even create a strategy.

Step #2: Review Competitors

As part of creating your marketing strategy, it's always good to review your competitors to see what they're doing and where you can find a competitive advantage. When reviewing your competitors, it's a good idea to also look at their performance. Where are they currently with their marketing, and what do you need to do to achieve similar results? For example, are they ranking on page #1 for a certain keyword that you should also be ranking on? Do they have more followers on LinkedIn than your brand? Their current performance can be a good benchmark for where you should aim and also give you an idea of what you need to do to get there.

Step #3: Create the Strategy

While I design the specific campaign, I keep this information in the back of my mind. What activities do I need to undertake to achieve those objectives while still sticking within the budget or any other constraints? How can we get the most within these boundaries?

Step #4: Define the actual KPIs

How will we know that we're moving in the right direction? What metrics will we track at each stage of the funnel and what metrics make sense for the activities we have planned? There's no sense in tracking a metric that you have no control over, as you'll be held accountable for your metrics. I sometimes see marketing teams that are responsible for KPIs like event attendees, but then either hasn't been given any budget for events or don't have any events planned. You don't want to make this mistake.

Examples of KPIs Across the Funnel

While the KPIs will depend on your planned strategy, you might look at the following KPIs. This strategy was focused on increasing brand awareness with specific sectors (that the brand had never worked in before) while also maintaining business-as-usual content to increase brand awareness around more general topics. Activities were focused on LinkedIn, SEO blog content, and in-person events (both hosting and attending) along with dedicated industry campaigns and the main objective: expanding into new sectors to increase overall deal size and, of course, drive revenue.

Top-of-Funnel: Awareness
- LinkedIn Followers: +10,000
- 10-20 Page 1 SEO ranking for target industries
- 20x conversations per month in the targeted sector with key audience

Mid-of-Funnel: Consideration

- 50–60 people per panel event
- Page 1 SEO ranking — digital experience agency

Bottom-of-Funnel: Traction

- 30x referrals
- 144 MQLs
- Deal size: increase 20 percent

AFTER YOU SET KPIS

Setting KPIs is only half the battle; once you've determined what KPIs you want to track, you then need to find a way to easily track these metrics, manage stakeholder expectations, and present your results. It's also important to review the KPIs regularly to make sure you're on track and can adjust if needed.

Tracking KPIs

You want to make tracking your KPIs as easy as possible. Most tools allow you to automate this process, and you should set this up as soon as possible so you can collect historical data and show the progress you're making over time. It can also be a good idea to create one central dashboard where you can show month-on-month results and help educate board members and other internal stakeholders on taking a more long-term approach to marketing.

Managing Stakeholder Expectations

Hopefully, you've involved your stakeholders in the process of defining the initial KPIs, and now it's just about continuing to manage these expectations. It's a fine line between making them feel heard when they have new ideas while also making sure it doesn't detract from the larger marketing strategy and that you have enough resources to execute these new ideas and the initial strategy. I often see the marketing manager or CMO as the driver of a van; they're driving toward the final destination, but there are lots of other people in the car who want to provide advice on the best routes. Some of these suggestions might be helpful, others may not, and it's your job to decide what ultimately fits your strategy and what should be politely ignored while still taking everyone on the journey with you.

Experimentation: Fail Fast, Fail Forward

Not all of your marketing will work or may not work as expected. Part of the value of tracking KPIs is to understand what is working and what is not and how you to adjust the strategy accordingly. It's important to embrace a growth mindset and be comfortable with some degree of failure. These campaigns and activations that don't work are just as valuable as they help you understand what doesn't resonate with your audience and offer insights to learn from. The faster you can learn from these mistakes, the stronger your marketing strategy will be.

Not all stakeholders will be comfortable with failure, especially the more risk-averse like CFOs. So, it can be helpful to have part of your marketing budget dedicated toward experimentation. This is where the less assured campaigns/approaches can go, and it can be seen as more of a gamble—awesome if it works, but equally okay if it doesn't.

While most B2C marketers will have an experimentation budget, I think everyone needs one. It allows you to be creative and try new approaches while also ensuring your CFO is on board.

PRESENTING RESULTS

Once you have determined and started tracking your KPIs, you need to ensure you present them regularly. I almost see KPIs and results as ways to talk about marketing and the work you're doing. They serve as a basis for structuring the conversation around and keeping internal stakeholders up to speed on your results.

Results should ideally be presented at board meetings at least once a quarter. Sometimes, boards don't have a spot on the agenda for marketing, but it's important to advocate for one. Even if you're only attending for 15-20 minutes to present the results, they need to know how their money is being spent and that it's a worthwhile investment not only to continue but also hopefully expand upon.

I also like to use these board reports as an opportunity to discuss any blockers. The board's main objective is to ensure the strategic direction of the company, and part of this is to ensure key initiatives can be undertaken. They have the power to help resolve these challenges, and they must know about any barriers preventing you from fully executing your strategy. Done tactfully, this can be a super-powerful approach to addressing challenges.

Between board meetings, it's helpful to keep stakeholders informed on results with regular reporting, which can be done via email or mini-strategy reviews. I recommend monthly reporting, even at a top level, to keep stakeholders up to date. This can be as simple as an email with the top three noteworthy results from that month, key steps for evolving your approach, and any additional "so what" items they should know about. Even if you don't receive responses or engagement on these emails, sharing the information is a good way to stay top of mind and raise awareness around your and your team's activities.

Getting Started with Your Marketing

"You have brains in your head and feet in your shoes. You can steer yourself in any direction you choose." —Dr. Seuss

Hopefully, this book has provided you with some key insights and actionable advice on how to start your marketing journey or expand on your existing activities. Regardless of where you are in your journey, it's never too early to start building brand awareness, as it's going to take time and consistent effort to get you where you want to go!

I meet many brands that are hesitant to get started because they don't have their proposition nailed or are worried about future changes. So, the one message I'd like to leave you with is not to let perfection stand in the way of your marketing.

Even with the best intentions, you're likely to make mistakes along the way, and you won't get everything right. I certainly haven't gotten everything right in building the CopyHouse brand and have made mistakes (both big and small) along the way. But making mistakes is how we learn, and by showing up and trying your best, you'll undoubtedly make progress toward having a recognizable brand that delivers regular, consistent leads and helps you achieve your bigger company objectives.

Best,
K.

www.ingramcontent.com/pod-product-compliance
Ingram Content Group UK Ltd.
Pitfield, Milton Keynes, MK11 3LW, UK
UKHW051043030325
4825UKWH00044B/515

9 781961 757813